Healing From The Loss Of A Parent

Adult Grief After A Parent Dies

Martina Roswell

© COPYRIGHT 2020 BY MARTINA ROSWELL

ALL RIGHTS RESERVED.

This Book is geared towards providing exact and reliable information in regard to the topic and issue covered. The publication is sold with the idea that the publisher is not required to render accounting, officially permitted, or otherwise, qualified services. If advice is necessary, legal or professional, a practiced individual in the profession should be ordered. From a Declaration of Principles which was accepted and approved equally by a Committee of the US Bar Association and a Committee of Publishers and Associations.

In no way is it legal to reproduce, duplicate, or transmit any part of this document in either electronic means or in printed format. Recording of this publication is strictly prohibited, and any storage of this document is not allowed unless with written permission from the publisher.

The information provided herein is stated to be truthful and consistent, in that any liability, in terms of inattention or otherwise, by any usage or abuse of any policies, processes, or directions contained within is the solitary and utter responsibility of the recipient reader. Under no circumstances will any legal responsibility or blame be held against the publisher for any reparation, damages, or monetary loss due to the information herein, either directly or indirectly.

Respective authors own all copyrights not held by the publisher. The information herein is offered for informational purposes solely and is universal as so. The presentation of the information is without a contract or any type of guarantee assurance.

The trademarks that are used are without any consent, and the publication of the trademark is without permission or backing by the trademark owner. All trademarks and brands within this book are for clarifying purposes only and are owned by the owners themselves, not affiliated with this document.

Table of Contents

Introduction 1

1. Emotional Reactions to Loss 4

2. The Truth about Grief 25

3. The Healing Power of Grief 38

4. Self-Destruction or Inner Strength 41

5. Uncovering Your Inner Strength 52

6. Vehicle for Growth 79

7. Yet Another Holiday 100

8. One Day at a Time 120

9. When the Glue Is Gone 133

10. When History Is All You Have Left 154

11. Grief and Spirituality 172

12. The Other Side of Grief 192

Conclusion..196

"When Your Dearly Beloved Parent Dies, It becomes a Memory and that Memory Becomes a Treasure"

Introduction

Your beloved parent dies, and strange things begin to happen to you. Grief manifests itself into something you are unfamiliar and uncomfortable with. You feel like you're lost at sea, and waves of different emotions continuously crash over you. You feel the current pushing you further away from the place you have known to be your normal.

All of a sudden, life disrupts your normal, and you find yourself sitting on the bench with grief. The loss of your beloved parent has taught you that death is a harsh reality to grasp. It feels like you are trapped in a disturbing dream you can't wake up from. Fear makes your heart stutter, your mind gets all worked up, and your brain screams for silence.

You can't take the depression any longer; you can't even look at the mirror without looking hard enough to try and recognize yourself. Your once happy disposition is now paled by sadness and grief. You remain lost under waves of crushing sadness, and you see no way of getting out of the situation. Grief isn't pretty. You will find it uncomfortable to sit with grief, and you may watch your grief journal gradually turn into a companion filled with your hidden emotions, and the truth about your broken heart.

There is nothing anyone can say to you after the death of your beloved parent that will bring them back and make your pain disappear. Know that you will sometimes stay up tossing and turning in your bed for half the night and you will sometimes have to force yourself to get out of bed in the morning. Things you used to be passionate about and enjoyed doing will feel like difficult tasks drying up the little energy you have. There will be changes in your appetite, and you may force yourself to eat and go out with friends just to fill up your social cup.

You may sometimes become an amazing actor; wear a brave face and a plastic smile so that everyone doesn't think you are crushed by the weight of your loss.

However, you are crushed by the weight of the lost on the inside.

Recognize that bereavement is a necessary aspect of living, just as death is an inevitable part of life. So, when death sits with you at your family table, and shock and its companions, tears, anger, hopelessness, and pain come knocking, you can still find a reason to live.

If you're confused about how to keep the family together when the glue is gone, and trying to wander over to the other side of grief, read on to know how to journey through your grief until you find yourself on the other side.

CHAPTER ONE
Emotional Reactions to Loss

Our beloved parent is no longer with us. Yes, I know. It appears like someone had ripped out your own heart or stolen part of your soul. These are normal and absolutely understandable sensations for those facing such an important loss. Often, we ask ourselves how much the life of our loved one is worth and how we can live without the sweet glace of our mother or the unconditional love of our father. They have always been there, ready to listen, support, and help us in any circumstance.

The reaction to the loss of our beloved parent upsets us. We all went through it, and it is part of our earthly existence. Our role as cherished eternal children suddenly changes. After the loss, we are there, sitting with ourselves, pondering who we are and what our role is. For many, it means assuring their children what our parents have left us - The love of a life. For others, in general, it is living in their memory and achieving goals that they would be proud of.

I know it personally. It is hard to recover from this shocking event. Our belief system and values are challenged as we search for meaning. We focus on the events that led to the loss. We try to understand the death and seek an answer to the question "Why".

Although everyone may react differently to the loss of a beloved parent, we can recognize some typical emotive reactions.

Shock and Emotional Numbness

The first response to our parent's death is usually shock. It acts as a protection for you from the intense feelings experienced after the traumatic event.

You may know that your parent has been down with an illness, and you may have been caring for them throughout their illness, but when they die, it always feels shocking and unbelievable.

As soon as a death occurs, experiences and conversations can be blurred due to shock from the loss. The period after the death is usually accompanied by a period of disbelief that the person has actually died. There is an overwhelming feeling of shock and disbelief. The feelings of the grief may not yet be intense as the news of the death hasn't really sunk in; you haven't really understood the reality of the death. You don't know how to respond to the news of the death. It feels like your life has been shaken from its place of comfort and turned upside down. At first, you may remain numb and carry on with your normal activities as if no one has died, when someone really important to you has died and is never coming back.

The numbness naturally protects you from the trauma. It will help you function well during the early stages after the death has occurred because you are detached from the reality of the loss. The people around you may be expecting you to feel intense suffering, but your behavior will leave them confused. It may feel off-balance, but as the days and weeks pass by, the shock and numbness will reduce, and you will start experiencing intense feelings until you become fully immersed in the grieving process.

The death of a beloved parent is hard to accept, and it may take a long time for you to understand the reality of the situation. You may feel like you have no purpose on earth. It takes time to heal from the loss of a parent. Sometimes, people become emotionally numb instead of experiencing a flood of emotions. Emotional numbness is when you feel nothing. You feel dead inside, as though you can't relate to the feelings of everyone else. Social interaction becomes a burden for you.

The death of your parent makes you sad, but you still find it difficult to recognize your emotions. Everyone else is crying and letting their feelings all out. Your friends visit you to comfort you and say things like, "we understand the pain you are going through at this time… your tears reflect the love and sadness in your heart". All of a sudden, you begin to feel guilty because you feel empty inside, and you don't have tears running down your face. You become worried that others will question your love for the person you have lost.

A sudden loss often triggers emotional numbness. The death of the person comes to you as a shock giving you no time to think about the possibilities of losing the person. Numbness, after a loved one dies, helps keep you from the reality of the person's death when you find it difficult to believe that the person has truly died. The emotional numbness is helpful to you as it gives your emotions time to catch up with what your mind has told you. You feel numb until you can accept the reality of the death. It protects you from insanity and helps you with your daily life activities.

Emotional numbness can give you distress and pain as you are unable to understand why you feel nothing after your loved one's death. It can leave you confused, and also affect your relationships with friends and relatives who may find your behavior surprising or annoying. Emotional numbness has a valuable purpose, as it protects you from breaking down after the traumatic experience of your loved one's death. Without the numbness, you would have felt the pain of the death strongly. The strain of the grief may have been too much for you to handle.

It is best to allow yourself to mourn. Try and talk about how you feel or write it down; it will help you through the numbness to your healing. Even though you may not feel like accepting support from your friends and family members, force yourself to accept it.

Sadness

If you have previously lost your first parent, it means that this is your second parent to die. It is a natural thing to feel very sorrowful at this stage. The death of your second parent also means that your children have lost both grandparents.

Transitioning into an adult orphan is painful. The parents that brought you into this world and loved you unconditionally have now left the world.

Mourn your loss. Don't try to fight the pain; allow yourself to embrace it.

Denial and Disbelief

Death is usually accompanied by a period of disbelief that the death is true. You feel like it is just a bad dream, and you keep hoping to wake up from the dream and find your loved one alive.

The conscious or unconscious refusal to accept the truth about the loss is known as denial.

There is a refusal to make the necessary preparations after the death, such as sorting through the person's belongings or filing the necessary paperwork.

You may still be leaving a space for your loved one after setting the dinner table, expecting they will walk to their usual seat at the table. You may sometimes dial their number, hoping they will pick up the phone. Instead, the brutal reality that they're never coming back stares you in the face.

Denial protects you against that brutal reality by giving you time to process everything that happened. It is your mind's way of protecting you from the pain of the death. It offers you a temporary break until you can accept the unwelcome reality of the death.

Denial is not a problem; it can only become a problem if it is done deliberately to avoid the reality of the loss.

There is a refusal to accept the fact of the death if you pretend your loved one traveled and would soon be home, get upset when anyone moves or changes the position of your loved one's belongings, or if you keep speaking to them as if they are still alive and can hear you.

You can cope with denial in several ways:

- Be truthful with yourself. Don't keep deceiving yourself about the reality of the situation. You need to come to terms with the loss and find a way to move on while treasuring their memory.

- Bring down the protective walls you have built to hide you from experiencing the pain of the loss and accept the truth of your pain.

- Accept what you have lost and take stock of what remains.

- Use words that are better representations of the truth of the situation; words like passed away or passed on should be replaced with words like died or dead.

- Visit the gravesite and places that remind you of your loved one. Allow yourself to be reminded about pleasurable and painful events in their lifetime. Confront the situation rather than avoiding it; it will shake you out of your denial.

- Don't hide your tears. Allow your children and others to see you crying. It will help them understand how much you miss the person, and they will also know that it is alright to mourn a loved one.

Confusion

The death of a loved one leaves you confused. You get confused about how the person can die. You think about it and say to yourself that you could have done something to prevent the person from dying.

Experiencing mental confusion after the death of your loved one is natural; you may feel like you experience the death of the person over and over again, and you don't even know which way is up.

It is natural and common to experience a wide range of confusing emotions at this time.

You don't know what to think and how to feel. You don't know how to move on with your life; your brain is simply confused about everything. You find yourself operating at half capacity because your brain is busy wondering where your loved one has gone.

You're confused about all the changes you are experiencing. You are confused about your relationship with other people. Some of the people you used to trust have disappeared after the death of your loved one, while some others act like the grief you are experiencing is a contagious disease. People may not acknowledge your loss, and even when they do, they don't know what to say to you.

You are confused about how to deal with all you are experiencing. You also have to be strong for your kids and other members of the family. Caring for your kids and supporting other members of your family is an issue for you because you are lying in bed with your shattered heart and unable to drag yourself out of bed. Your dreams have been destroyed. You are confused about the future; it seems uncertain because your dreams have been crushed beyond recognition.

The world is a different place without your loved one, and life without them is unimaginable; this is confusing.

Relief

You may feel relief and grief simultaneously after the death of a parent you have been caring for. This feeling is not only natural but inevitable, and it doesn't mean that you don't miss your parent. You love and miss them dearly.

If your parent was sick for an extended period before finally giving up, you are sad that they died, but it is also natural for you to feel relief at the end of their suffering. Your feeling of relief is a show of your love for them as their sickness will no more continue.

You may sometimes feel terrible about feeling relieved. You feel as if you wanted your parent to die, but that's not the case. You are happy to have reached the finished line of a race you weren't sure you possessed the ability to complete.

The feeling of relief only signifies pride that you fulfilled your commitment to the end. Relief is not regretting.

Guilt

Guilt is another common reaction after the death of a parent. Some people who have lost a loved one may say they feel they are directly or indirectly responsible for the death of the person. Guilt may be part of your grieving process if you feel like you didn't do enough to help the person during their lifetime. You can also feel guilty if your relationship with the deceased was a difficult one.

You may feel guilty if your parent died, and you did not have a smooth relationship with them during their lifetime. Your relationship may have been rocky or distant. When you get hit by the reality of your parent's death, you start wishing that you should have said some nice things to them while they were alive.

You ponder on the hurtful things you said and did to them while they were alive, then you wish you could unsay and undo those things. You wish you had spent more time and created good memories with them. Guilt and regret are also normal responses to the death of a loved one.

Don't be too harsh on yourself. The feelings are a normal part of grief. It is best to find someone who will listen to you speak as you pour out your heart. Don't try to repress the painful feelings. The emotions may seem strange but working through the feelings as they are is essential to your healing.

Anger

After the death of a parent, you may feel anger toward them because their loving relationship with you has been prematurely cut off. Bereaved people are prone to anger.

Anger is a natural emotion that is a part of the grieving process. You can get angry when you feel that a person died before their time. You may get angry when you had plans for the future together with your parent, but they suddenly died before the time the plans were meant to be carried out.

You may also be angry at yourself for things you said or didn't say to your parent while they were alive. You may feel angry at your parent or angry at yourself for things you did or didn't do.

Depression

Grief turned into bereavement-related depression is more than just sadness. It is a painful condition that is capable of taking away the mourner's will to remain alive; this is the reason you mustn't bottle up your feelings when your loved one dies.

If you hide your feelings and don't let it out, it will grow into a severe depression which is capable of taking lives. If you dwell too much on your negative emotions, you are at the risk of falling into long-term depression.

You don't have to worry about your feelings. Distraction away from your situation is a great strategy to protect yourself from depression. Engage in activities you enjoy and do things that will keep you busy and take your mind away from your situation. Hang out with a friend; go shopping together; see a movie together.

Don't attempt to reduce your depression by getting drunk on alcohol; heavy drinking will only keep you depressed for a longer period of time.

Avoid negative distractions like driving out and over speeding. Also, avoid sitting down, worrying, and talking about how bad your life would be without your parent.

The intense feelings of grief you suffer when you lose a parent can lead to depression. For those who already have depression issues, it can make their depression worse. Some people feel like there is no reason for them to remain alive after a painful death because life is no longer meaningful to them.

Bereavement-related depression has outward signs that are similar to other types of depression.

- **Exhibiting mood changes**

Depression convinces you that you must remain sad and never be happy; this is the reason a once cheerful and happy person can get easily upset with people and push them away, so they can stay alone and remain sad. They just don't want to be happy.

Other family members may not realize your new behavior as depression; they may just think that you have gone weird since the death of your parent.

- **Social isolation**

Depression is isolating. When you lose a beloved parent, you may start isolating yourself from people you used to be close to. Whenever you get close to them, the depression in your heart gives you a warning signal, telling you that those people will be taken away someday.

It is normal that as we age, we'll have increased recognition of mortality, and we cannot pretend that we're going to live forever. Bereavement-related depression makes you isolate yourself from people.

Since depression causes social isolation, social contact can help treat your depression.

- **Insomnia**

You may have to relearn your entire life when you lose a loved one. Sleeping is one of the things you have to relearn when relearning new ways of taking care of yourself after a loss.

You are tired and exhausted, but you can't sleep. Even though you've never been an insomniac before, you find yourself staying up all through the night.

Sleeplessness after a loss should not be ignored. You feel frustrated because you want to sleep, but you can't sleep; this makes the situation worse.

If you are experiencing sleeplessness in your grief, it should not be ignored even though insomnia is considered a common reaction during the grieving process.

Aging adults may have been known to have more sleep problems, but this inability to sleep is also more intense in people suffering from the loss of a loved one.

You can help yourself relax before bed; doing some conscious relaxation will help you calm your mind. Listening to soothing natural sounds as you fall asleep will help you bridge the gap between wakefulness and sleep and give you a good night's rest.

- **Loss of identity**

I don't know who I am anymore. Sounds familiar, right?

Our identity is created from our own perception of ourselves. Our identity is formed and shaped through our relationships, the media, our culture, and our individual experiences. We aren't consciously aware of our identity, but it shapes our existence.

Grief-related depression can lead to a sudden loss of self-worth or ego. It can make you suddenly stop caring about doing the things you used to enjoy doing, caring about your appearance, your health, or even what you eat.

- **Yearning**

Yearning is a feeling of intense longing or desire for something or someone. Grief takes yearning to the next level. It strips you of other desires.

The chief symptom of grief after the death of a loved one is yearning. A common experience for many people is sometimes thinking that they are seeing the person or hearing their voice. You may find yourself constantly thinking about everything that happened towards the end of the person's life.

You have an intense desire to have them back; you experience an intense emotional state of yearning. It takes time for you to accept the reality of their death. You try to hold on to the things particular to them. You keep looking for them in places where they used to be until your brain begins to realize that they're never coming back.

The way other people sometimes react to you when you are bereaved can be confusing. Some people may simply avoid you because they feel your pain but honestly do not know what to say to console you. Their behavior may be difficult for you to understand because you may want to discuss things about the deceased with them, but you will feel like they have already forgotten the person.

You may not be prepared for the mood swings that accompany grief but remember that the pain you feel will ease as time goes on.

You do not need to mourn them forever, but you will cherish their memories forever.

CHAPTER TWO
The Truth about Grief

Grief is overpowering. It can rewrite your address book and create a distance between you and your friends or relatives. Even though grief is not exclusively about the physical death of an individual, it is sometimes used interchangeably with bereavement. It may take you a few months or even years to work through your grief.

Grief demands to be felt. One moment you may feel like you have finally gotten over the death of the person, but the next moment you are right back to your grief. Even if you succeed at making it past the day without the feeling of grief, it can come back to you at bedtime, making you toss and turn at night.

Grief gradually finds its way into your heart, soaks up all the energy in your body, and steals your peace away. Grief isn't there to only make you suffer and cause you pain; it comes to show you a truth about your life. It makes you know how deeply you cared about your loved one and how much you value them.

The Grieving Process

Grieving usually begins with denial. Denial helps to lessen the impact the death would have on you so that it won't be too overwhelming for you. It protects you and gradually fades away until you can face the reality of the loss.

You may succeed in suppressing your grief, but it usually comes up again when you have forgotten about it.

Some people lose themselves on the path of grief, but you don't have to. Some deaths are so painful that people will understand, and no one will judge you even if you decide to keep walking on the path of grief.

If you decide to get out of the path of grief, there is a better path to walk on.

Fear and Anxiety

There are different stages of grief, but there's another part of grief that is not usually talked about. Fear is that part of grief that can be triggered by a loss.

Some people experience the fear of the unknown future, the fear of their own mortality, the fear of being alone, or the fear of how they will go through life without their loved one. Some even experience the fear that they would see their loved one's ghost, and the fear of going into their bedroom or even walking past it.

We sometimes experience an element of shame in the fear of the unknown. We don't want to talk about the fear we feel because someone might think we're crazy if we shared our fears with them.

Anxiety is experienced after the death of a loved one. Feeling like you have lost your sense of safety and control in life when your loved one dies is a normal part of the grieving process. Anxiety is common during grief. You may feel worried and scared that you may lose someone else in the future.

Medium for Communication

Your desire to communicate with your loved one grows after their death. You are constantly thinking about where they are and what they are doing. You want them to be in a better place and be happy. You want to receive a message from them or talk to them and ask them questions. There are times when you just imagine yourself having a beautiful moment with them, so it brings tears to your eyes. When we are grieving, people who claim to communicate with the dead can prey on our vulnerability. We may be tempted to seek mediums who claim to communicate with the dead to give us messages from our loved ones.

It's natural to crave the attention of your loved one when you are missing them, but don't go seeking a medium who will tell you certain things your loved one says you should do to guide you along the path of your life.

No emotion is useless

All emotions are useful; none is useless. They may not make you feel good about yourself, but they are not useless. We don't want to feel the emotion of sadness, but we feel it from time to time. When we lose a loved one, we feel sad. We may also feel guilty when we think of events that led to the person's death. We may feel guilty that we should have done more for them, and maybe they would have still been alive. We didn't want them to die.

The death of a loved one leaves us flooded with emotions. We may be disturbed by guilt if we were present or not present when they died. If we were also in the same situation that led to their death, we might even be plagued by survivor's guilt. When we are having a good time with our friends, we suddenly remember our loved one; then, our happiness turns into sadness and guilt. We may even decide to stay at home away from friends or events after the person's death.

Guilt is an emotion that may come after the death of a loved one, and you don't have to feel guilty for being happy. It's evident that no therapist can take away your feelings, but you can take their advice to help you cope with the loss.

Go through your grieving process, knowing that no emotion is useless. The emotions are useful to help you go through the process. Every emotion you feel comes as a result of the loss, and as you express them and not hide them, you will heal with time.

Morbid Thoughts

After your loved one's death, you think about their condition and if they can feel anything. You wonder if they can see that they're being buried, you wonder if they come to the house after their death, you wonder if they would like to be buried with their favorite things, and you may sometimes think that they may not be really dead, and will come back to life just before they are buried. As time passes after their burial, you think about what their body may look like now.

Stages of Grief

The grieving process has no road map for it. Most people go through stages of grief, but it doesn't mean that you must progress from stage 1 to stage 2, and so on. You go through the stages at different times, depending on the events taking place in your life; there is no linear progression.

You can visit different stages when you remember your loved one; during events like birthdays or anniversaries, sadness or depression can take over your heart. You can visit any of the stages years after their death.

The Kubler-Ross model talks about five stages of grief. **Let's argument the five stages of grief.**

1. Denial

The first stage of grief is denial. It involves shock, avoidance, fear, avoidance, confusion, and elation. When you lose a parent, there is an initial period of disbelief and shock. Shock is defined as a sudden, surprising, or upsetting experience or event.

Denial is a defense mechanism. It involves the refusal to accept reality or a situation that is too much to handle. It is too uncomfortable for you, so you reject the fact even though you may have overwhelming evidence before you. At this stage of the process, you refuse to accept the reality of your loved one's death, and you may be unable to partake in your usual activities. You cling to your preferable reality. You believe that a mistake has been made in the diagnosis, and your parent can still come back to life somehow.

You can't believe that they're really dead, so you say things like, "this can't be happening to me."

Denial is used by many people to avoid dealing with the painful feelings associated with the death of their loved one.

2. Anger

The second stage of grief is anger. It involves

frustration, anxiety, and irritation. Frustration begins to set in when you realize that your parent has truly died and is not coming back. You can't continue to deny the fact of the loss, so feelings of abandonment and helplessness start to take over you.

You acknowledge the loss, but you begin to ask questions like, "why would this happen?"; "who is to blame for this?"; "this isn't fair". You become angry at yourself, at the doctor, at other individuals, at God, and even at life. Anger is an intense emotional state involving a strong feeling of annoyance, displeasure, or hostility.

3. Bargaining

The third stage of grief is bargaining. It involves telling one's story, reaching out to others, and struggling to find meaning.

The bargaining is about negotiating with a higher being that you feel has the power to prevent the loss or change the situation. You think about things that should have been done differently to prevent the loss. You have hope of preventing the loss, so you start making deals with God hoping that the condition would change and your loved one would remain alive if they are close to dying, or that they would come back to life if they have already died.

To save a terminally ill parent's life, you may bargain for an extended life for them and promise God that you will turn from your old ways of living and become a better person.

4. Depression

The fourth stage of grief is depression. It is characterized by persistent feelings of sadness, loss of interest, loneliness, helplessness, self-pity, difficulty in concentration, changing appetites, and sometimes suicidal thoughts.

Depression is a mood disorder affecting a person's well-being. Activities that used to make you happy whenever you partook in them now feel different to you; you no longer have the feeling of pleasure those activities used to give you.

Depression is a normal reaction to the loss of a loved one. You realize what has happened, but it's too difficult to bear. Things are just the way they are. You feel an emptiness in your heart, and sadness spreads its arms around you.

5. Acceptance

Acceptance is the fifth stage of grief. It is characterized by a sense of hope, adjusting to the new reality, and moving on. Acceptance involves consenting to receive something offered to you. It is your assent to the reality of the loss without trying to change it. In this fifth stage, you embrace the inevitable future and say things like, "there is nothing I can do to change the fact of the loss"; "everything is going to be alright".

Time has passed, and you now feel at peace with the situation. You are no longer weighed down by the extreme sadness the death has caused you.

Symptoms of Grief

Grief has symptoms that are often misunderstood. People have different symptoms of grief depending on their relationship with their parent who died and other emotional factors they may be experiencing at the time of the loss. Grief shakes our whole being. It gets to us physically, touches our emotions, affects our social lives, and also touches us on a spiritual level.

You should understand the symptoms of grief as it will help you during your period of grieving.

It is normal for your emotions to change. You experience peace and then become sad again.

Grief has physical, emotional, social, and spiritual symptoms.

Physical

Physical symptoms of grief include experiencing stomach aches, headaches, pains, fatigue, sleep disorder, getting involved in self-destructive activities, an increase or decrease in appetite, crying, and sighing.

Social

Social symptoms of grief include clinginess, loneliness, and isolation from others.

Emotional

Emotional symptoms of grief include sadness, guilt, anxiety, irritability, frustration, anger, confusion, yearning, depression, feeling a lack of control, feelings of distraction, and unstable emotions.

Spiritual

Spiritual symptoms of grief include redirection and closeness to God, getting angry at God for allowing the death of your parent, questioning your faith, and asking questions about the meaning of life.

CHAPTER THREE
The Healing Power of Grief

Could grieving help us heal ourselves and the world?

We tend to run away from our grief. Sometimes we hide our grief and act like everything is fine when it's actually not. We have learnt right from our childhood days that we should control our emotions, but how do we do it in our time of grief. The pain of grief is so shattering that we find it difficult to control it; we can get ourselves distracted from it for some time, but the feelings always come flooding back in no time.

After we have walked the path of our own grief, the experience will help us better understand the pain of others, and how to react to them in their time of grief. It can make us better companions to them. Since we have experienced the same situation as them, we know what to say to them or what to do to help them heal from the grief associated with their loss. We find it easier to guide them through the process.

Grief can help us heal ourselves and the world.

A Chance to Heal Our Deepest Wounds

Grief can help us heal our deepest wounds. After the occurrence of traumatic events, people often share their sorrows even if they have not been directly affected by the traumatic events. Receiving tributes from people is an essential part of your healing process. It helps remind you of all the good things your loved one has done and builds a foundation for your healing.

Don't try to get out of your grief prematurely; resisting it will only make matters worse; it will extend your grieving period as you will still carry the hurtful emotions that will prevent you from healing. Your deepest wounds will be healed if you don't hold back; allow yourself to freely experience your grief.

The Pressure to Move On

Born with the natural ability to grieve, we can cry when we are tensed. There is no fixed duration of time that you have to grieve for.

Friends and relatives may start pressurizing you to move on with your life. They may say things like, "aren't you done with your grieving?"

Even though there is no timeline for grieving, we hide our sorrow instead of letting it out because we don't want it to make the people around us feel uncomfortable.

Suppressing our grief can be destructive while expressing our grief helps us heal our deepest wounds. Once we open up, we can tap into the creative force of our emotions and inspire the world.

CHAPTER FOUR
Self-Destruction or Inner Strength

Life is a game, so learn to play skillfully. If you lose at something, simply laugh it off and try again.

There is a difference between going through the pain associated with grief and adding more pain to the already unbearable pain.

I have seen many people create more pain in their desire to run away from the pain they are experiencing. How can life be killing you, and you help in killing yourself too?

The loss of a loved one makes a lot of people lose their identity and become self-destructive. As they try to numb their pain, they start getting into self-destructive activities.

I have seen so many willing to take any road to escape the pain they are experiencing, thereby increasing their pain physically, emotionally, and mentally. When the denial phase is over, and they are faced with the reality of the loss, they try self-destructive activities.

You have been taught how to love, but you haven't been taught how to heal. You can't be held; your voice is slowly disappearing from your cries. You look around, and isolation is your only company. You have sat in silence with your emotions of loss and watched pain taking you down the inevitable path of unbearable sorrow, so you created room for pain's manifestations to lead you into self-destruction.

The best we can do for a grieving person is to give them our presence in their time of need. When they feel isolated and lost, they need someone to draw them close and tell them that everything is going to be alright.

The pain of loneliness and emptiness of separation is capable of leading the griever to self-destruction. Some people decide to push those who want to be there for them in their time of grief away, and then they sit alone with their pain. They want everyone to leave them alone so they can be alone even though being alone is painful for them. They are then left alone to choose either the path to self-destruction or healing.

The best way to heal from pain is to go through the pain without holding back. Our struggles should be seen as a source of strength. Whenever we are faced with adversity, we must remember that they come to make us stronger.

Sometimes in the face of adversity, it is almost impossible to stay positive, but you can still find inner strength and peace in moments of grief if you look positively at your struggles. Be reminded that they are giving you the opportunity for growth.

You Are Strong Enough

You are strong enough to cope with life's necessary ups and downs. We get a chance to see how strong we are when we are left with the only choice of being strong.

Our capacity for hardship is flexible like bamboo. You can build your resilience, which is the capacity to recover quickly from hardships. Resilience is not a fixed trait; it takes time to build. Resilience is sometimes taken as mental toughness. Being resilient does not mean that you won't experience stress or pain; it means working through the pain.

Changing your mindset and certain behaviors can help you develop flexibility and help you build resilience. You don't have to be afraid of bending once in a while. When you allow yourself to bend and return to your former self, you'll be stronger than you used to be.

We may have been taught while we were growing up that all pain is harmful, and this makes some people resort to self-destruction in an attempt to escape the pain.

You must know that experiencing pain is a part of life, and you will feel pain even if your parent's death was anticipated. We may try to hide our pain, but we will find it difficult dealing with the pains of life if we're afraid to feel it. We should wear our pain willingly. It is meant to expose our weakness and help us crush our troubles.

If the death of your parent was sudden and unexpected, you are left shocked. You are overwhelmed because the loss is so disruptive that your capacity to adapt is tested.

In the case of sudden death, there was no time for a gradual transition for you to make some changes. All of a sudden, your security is taken away without any notice, and your expectations are violated. You are left with a big gap that you don't know how to fill. You can only think about the world with your parent alive, but now there is emptiness where they used to be. You aren't ready to face the unbelievable reality because there was no time for you to gradually absorb the reality of the change. The world you used to know has been suddenly disrupted.

You may feel like you are unable to continue living due to the extreme feelings of anxiety and depression you are suffering. Your sense of control has been snatched away.

Even when a death is anticipated, these issues still confront you, but in this case, you had a period of anticipation that made the death predictable. You experience pain when your parent dies, but you were prepared to receive the news, and you also know the cause of death.

You were able to tell your parent that you love them and also had time to discuss issues before their death. There was also time to finish doing things or to create a new path for the things you started with them. You were able to do the special things you wanted to do for them before their death. You experience the painful emotions associated with losing a loved one, but your coping capacity has already been trained to deal with the flooding emotions; this kind of anticipated loss makes sense.

The loss associated with a sudden death makes no sense. The sudden shock from the loss of losing your parent without any warning makes it difficult to understand the implications of what has happened. Acceptance can become an issue even if you recognize the occurrence of the death.

Since you were not ready for the death, you continuously replay the events that led to your parent's death in your mind and try to make sense of everything that happened, but you may be unable to point out where things went wrong.

When you look back at the events leading up to their death, you may discover that you missed the clues that could have prevented the loss. You may discover that there were actually signs that your loved one wasn't feeling too well if they died suddenly without a prolonged period of illness.

You may also discover that they were visiting people they hadn't seen for a long time and wanted to finish up important unfinished businesses.

Your mind takes on the task of trying to piece together all the information to give you a sense of anticipation; this will help you reduce your feelings of shock when you find some missed clues that your parent was going to die. You begin to say things like, "maybe he knew he was going to die" "he started talking to us more about family love and unity between siblings."

This understanding of the situation makes the loss more bearable. It gives you a sense of perception and control over the situation, providing you with a sense of anticipation and preparation.

However, you encounter problems when you start judging yourself and holding yourself responsible for not acting on the clues you received. Most grievers feel terribly bad about this.

Even though they are not physicians to run tests on their parent to see if anything was wrong with them, some grievers still live with the guilt of not recognizing that their parent had a hidden illness. They react emotionally to the loss as they feel that they didn't take care of their responsibilities. Symptoms of grief tend to be more intense and long-lasting for individuals whose parents died sudden deaths.

The reality that your world has been drastically altered demoralizes you as you try to cope with the additional stress that leaves you exhausted. Issues like not having time to say goodbye to your loved one, or not finishing unfinished business weigh you down. You wish that you could have at least said some last words to them, told them you loved them, and bade them farewell.

You may lose confidence in life. You learn to treat your living loved ones better because you have been taught a valuable lesson of life that your loved ones can be snatched away at any time without warning.

Studies have shown that widows whose husbands died sudden deaths were less likely to remarry as they are unwilling to experience the loss of another husband to them, and father to their children.

Some people live with the consequences of the sudden death throughout their lifetime, some others never have their confidence and sense of security return to them, and some others have less dramatic consequences.

Remember that you are strong enough to go through the pain. Build your resilience, and you will smile again.

Strength From Within

Other people might be far away from you when you need them most. They might also be there but won't be able to support you the way you want them to. In times like this, you will need to draw strength from within to help you during your grief.

Your belief in the existence of God or a higher source of energy can help you draw strength from within. Meditation can help you draw strength from within. Books and online sources can also give you the strength you need at this time of your loss.

Your local library or friends can give you information about the books to read. Many spiritual books and teachers have been inspiring to many who are grieving, and you will find them helpful too.

Don't zip your mouth shut; reach out to friends, and they will point you in the direction of the sources that will provide you with the needed inspiration to move on with your life after the loss.

CHAPTER FIVE
Uncovering Your Inner Strength

Even if an elderly parent has lived a long life, no amount of preparation can make the death easier on you. We know that many logistical details have to be sorted out after our loved one's death; some of these include the funeral arrangements, the finances, and helping your surviving parent go through their grieving process.

Age does not excuse the fact that the death of a loved one leaves our hearts broken and changes our lives. Despite the fact that your parent lived a long life on earth, you are still being affected by their death.

You will be worried about issues like how your children will handle the death of their grandparent and even worried about taking too much time off from work; you have to do all these while staying strong and putting on a brave face for your family.

The topic is a difficult one to discuss because it is a painful reality that a lot of people are going through.

Coping with the death of your beloved parent may be painful, but here are some tips to help make the transition a little easier on you.

Following these steps will help you go through the grieving process, uncover your strength, and you will find happiness again.

Forgive Yourself

No parent-child relationship is perfect, so you shouldn't let guilt weigh you down after your parent's death. You may have had some arguments or issues with your parent while they were alive; the guilt from that can become a burden for you after their death. You may feel guilty that you didn't do enough to help them during their lifetime.

Realize that whatever has happened is in the past. It's not strange for mistakes and disputes to occur between parents and children. Your parents still loved you even if they didn't say it to you all the time.

By recognizing that the past should remain the past, you accept that it's unchangeable. You can begin to allow yourself to get over the guilt you feel and think about all the good times you have shared with your loved one. Stick to the good times; your parent would want you to remember them.

Face Your Feelings

If feelings of anger are left to grow stronger, it can add to your stress during your period of grief. Explore your feelings and meditate. Practicing meditation will help you understand your feelings better.

Grief influences our emotions. Imagine yourself going to sit on a riverbank just to watch boats sailing by. In the same way, by watching your thoughts, you'll discover that grief also influences your emotions. When you watch your thoughts, it creates an awareness of their impact; the power of emotions can be reduced by anticipating them.

Keep Talking

It is a painful thing not to be able to speak with your beloved parent anymore; this harsh reality is difficult to accept. Sometimes, you talk to them even though you know you won't hear them answer you. You may ask them what their thoughts on issues are; it's just a way for you to get the words you want to say to them out.

If it makes you feel comfortable to visit their grave and talk to them in your thoughts, then do it. It helps you keep their memory alive and also helps you keep your feelings in check.

Look After Yourself

Grief can affect you in many ways. Since it can cause changes in appetite, sleep disorders, and problems with the immune system, you need to protect your health and stay fit.

Before you attempt to show others how to care for their health, care for yours first. Protect your health first to ensure that you are capable of helping others protect themselves; just like the pre-flight safety instructions, put on your own oxygen mask before showing others how to do it.

You mustn't take big steps; small steps are okay too. Stay hydrated; ensure you eat natural, unprocessed foods. Go on walks with friends; it will keep you healthy and fit.

Take Time Out

The arrangements after the death are physically and mentally exhausting. An overwhelming to-do list awaits you; addressing legal matters and the funeral arrangements are some issues to be taken care of. You must look after your physical and mental health.

A vacation would be great to help you recuperate after things have settled. Taking time off shouldn't make you feel guilty; you'll return home rested and refreshed.

Avoid Comparisons

Our self-consciousness may increase during grief; we become highly self-conscious of how others see us. The way you look or behave mustn't be in a particular way, so you shouldn't judge your reaction to the loss.

You may return to work immediately after your parent's burial, and people will say why did you return to work so soon? You may also decide to take several weeks off, and people will say you took too much time off.

You don't have to return to work when people feel it is right for you to; don't worry about what they might think about you. This journey is yours alone, so you alone should be the judge; just do what you feel is right for you.

Be Patient

It's natural to miss a loved one, so you'll need time to get used to missing them. Time can heal the pain, but you may still continue missing your beloved parent even after five years. The pain associated with missing them, however, decreases with time. Recovery will happen gradually, so don't waste your time trying to force the healing to take place quickly.

Support Your family

The news of a parent's death can send shock waves across the whole family. It may make us grieve but remain withdrawn and not notice others are also grieving.

Lend a helping hand to other family members, and you won't feel isolated. When you help others cope, you will also feel better. When you form a team with your family members, you can support each other through the grieving period.

Enjoy Precious Memories

There will be times when you will find it difficult to stop thinking about your parent. You may even find yourself holding back tears at work when colleagues offer their condolences.

You can still enjoy your beloved parent's company by remembering the good memories and the happy times you shared with them. Relive the precious moments you shared with them. You can see them in your mind's eye whenever you wish. Continue to keep them alive in your thoughts. With time, you will be able to remember them with a smile on your face.

Accept the New You

Our perspective and opinions about life change as we get older. The passing of a parent changes you; it increases your tolerance level. Grief increases your awareness of change. You may be someone who gets easily annoyed when you go late to an event, miss a given deadline, or even have a gadget malfunction. Grief helps you understand that all things change, so you are prompted to prioritize what is really important. Issues that used to annoy you then begin to pale into insignificance.

Value your time and enjoy every moment of it. Grab each day with happiness and gratitude, and let the new you live out your passion.

Reach Out To Others for Support

Hard work seems less burdensome when others lend you a helping hand. Grieving the loss of your loved one may be the hardest work you have ever done, so reaching out to others for support is perhaps the most compassionate thing you can do for yourself at this time.

Elders are a source of great wisdom, experience, and love. Some people see elders as people who have outlived their usefulness and are no more useful, so they may not fully acknowledge your loss if your parent was old.

When an elderly person dies, you should say things like, "your mother was a nice person; you must miss her so much; I'm sorry for your loss" instead of things like, "you should be thankful that your mother lived a long life. Let her go in peace".

If the person who has died wasn't your biological parent but was a parent-figure to you, you still have the right to mourn them fully. It is normal for you to go through the grieving process.

Blended or nontraditional family members can bring about disenfranchised grief, which is the grief that a person experiences when the loss they incurred is one that they cannot acknowledge openly or mourn publicly.

Reach out and express yourself to people who understand your feelings and will give you time to pour out your feelings of grief. Avoid judgmental people or those who try to talk you into repressing your feelings. Sharing your pain with others doesn't mean that it will immediately disappear, and you will be free from the pain of grief; it only means that with time, the pain will become more bearable for you.

When you reach out to others for support, it builds your connection to them and, in turn, strengthens the bond you share with them. Your life will become livelier if you connect with others.

Respect Your Physical and Emotional Limits

It is crucial that you respect your physical and emotional limits. After the loss, you may be unable to think clearly, and your ability to make decisions may be impaired. You will definitely be left fatigued by your feelings of sadness, so strive to lighten your schedule as much as possible.

Pay attention to what your mind and body are saying to you. Low energy will slow you down, so look after yourself and get enough rest. Ensure that you eat balanced meals.

Understand that if you are to heal, you must mourn. Do not overwork your brain by thinking about the death all through the day. Be friendly to your brain.

Embrace Your Spirituality

Some people may tell you that with faith, you don't need to grieve. Well, that's not true. Don't believe their words. Express your faith in ways that you want to.

You may be angry with God for allowing your beloved parent to die; this feeling is a normal part of grief. Spend time with people who understand your religious beliefs and show their support; people who won't criticize you for the feelings you are expressing.

You need to speak out about your feelings even with your personal faith; your beliefs don't stop you from exploring your thoughts and feelings. Problems will build up inside you if you suppress your grief, so express your grief even as you express your faith.

Allow Yourself to Search for Meaning

You may ask questions such as "what happens after death?" "Where is my loved one now?" Realize that questions about life and its meaning are common and normal after a death. Important questions like these should be asked. Even if you don't find the answers you are anticipating, allow yourself the opportunity to think, feel, and ask questions.

Treasure Your Memories

Your beloved parent still lives on in spirit through your memories, even though they are no longer living with you physically on earth. Treasure the memories and remember to share them with others.

Memories can trigger feelings in you that will make you laugh or even cry. Death may have stolen your beloved parent from you, but no one can steal your memories of the times you shared with them. You can also create lasting tributes to honor your special bond with them.

Move Toward Your Grief And Heal

If you want to get over your grief and be happy again, you mustn't avoid mourning the death of your parent. Openly express your grief to help you with your healing. Go through the process of grief; denying it will make your life more confusing. Move toward your grief, and you will heal in no time.

Getting over your grief will not happen overnight because grief is a process and not an event. You need patience and tolerance at this time. The death of your parent may have brought changes into your life, but know that everything will be okay.

After the death of a parent, the bereaved may feel pressured to stay strong and put on a brave face, which prevents you from going through the grieving process properly.

Some people believe that grief has an expiry date. They think that you should grieve for a period of time, and then you must get over the loss at a particular time; this belief isn't right. Grief can take months or even years. It shows up in different forms. Honor your own timetable and let it run its course.

Share Your Feelings

Most people who have suffered a loss keep the feelings trapped within them and choose not to deal with it openly. It is a mistake to bottle up the feelings; they will end up coming out in unhealthy ways.

Consider sharing your feelings with your friends and family members. Joining a support group will be highly beneficial to you. Help yourself lighten your weight by sharing your grief with your relatives and friends.

We are designed to connect with others when we are stressed because we are social creatures. We are designed to share both the good and the bad stuff that happens to us in life.

Choose Your Confidantes Wisely

It is wise to open up, but it is even wiser to choose your confidantes wisely. It is not everyone that you should open up to; be selective about who you open up to.

There will be people who only want to show you how to grieve or only want you to take their own advice on how to grieve. Learn how to deal wisely with them. They may think it is their duty to protect you from your grief, but that will only hinder you from going through the grief process, and it will delay your healing.

Choose people who will listen to you speak about your feelings and will stand by you, so you don't have to go through the pain alone. Good listeners are great for this.

Grieve With Your Children

Be free to allow your children see that the death of your parent has left you upset. It is also their grandparent who has died. They may also miss their grandparent, but if you keep acting as if nothing has happened, they will also hold back their feelings, and this is not the healthy way to go.

Their feelings will be normalized when they see that you're also grieving. They will learn from you that they can grieve and still live their life, even if they don't feel like moving on. Help them understand that it is okay for them to express their feelings of sadness while grieving after a death occurs.

Respect Traditions but Be Aware Of Triggers

There are events or things that will trigger your feelings more than others during your grieving period. Family gatherings and holidays are events that are sure to trigger your feelings. It is wise to let your friends and relatives know that these events or moments can get to you emotionally, so they can understand your feelings and be supportive of you.

Family life has different traditions. In the wake of a loss, there are new ways to cope with these traditions. You can either do the things the deceased used to do so that you can honor their memory, or you can replace the old traditions with new traditions. You can cook your loved one's favorite meal at home, or even go out to eat at their favorite restaurant.

When you do what they enjoyed doing while they were on earth, and create new traditions, things will begin to work out well. Instead of sticking to family traditions that will cause you more pain after your loved one's death, create a new tradition to replace the old one. You can decide to travel elsewhere for Thanksgiving or Christmas, as opposed to spending those times at your parent's house. Just keep trying new things to see which works best for you.

Seek Help

Help can be received from a support group, and a one-on-one therapy session will be highly beneficial. There are numerous trained therapists who offer counseling and assistance to those grieving after the death of their loved one. Support groups for people mourning their loved ones can be found online. In-person and online supports will help you through the grieving process.

Whichever you choose, they both serve the purpose of allowing you the freedom to discuss your feelings in a safe space and get great advice that will help you cope.

Be Understanding

Since everyone processes grief differently, show understanding and love towards your surviving parent, children, or other members of the family.

Some people like to grieve privately while keeping themselves busy. Some may choose to mask their grief and work towards making everyone laugh away their sorrows.

A zero-judgmental mentality is important during grief because not everyone is visibly emotional while grieving; some grieve silently, and it doesn't mean that they're not grieving at all.

Give Yourself a Break

It is wise to give yourself a break after the loss. You don't have to sort through your loved one's belongings immediately after their death. You don't have to take on every task either. If things get too painful, give yourself time to relax and breathe. You can store your parent's belongings in a safe place until you are physically and emotionally ready to sort through it.

Get Organized

It doesn't feel right to be worried about money at a difficult time like this. Even though you have bills to pay, and financial documents to keep track of after your parent's death, worrying about money may still feel like a taboo to you.

It is best to create a space in your home that is dedicated to going through financial and legal matters. Ensure that you clean up after the mess; don't leave messy papers lying on the dining room table. You can also choose to invest in a paper organizer so that all the documents are organized, and you won't have to keep looking for documents that should have been appropriately arranged.

Don't Forget To Take Care of Yourself

One thing you must remember to do is to take care of yourself amidst everything. You may be too busy taking care of everyone else, putting on a brave face, and ensuring that all arrangements are properly made, but neglect yourself in the act. Remember to set some time aside for yourself. Grief can be emotionally, physically, and mentally exhausting, so go on a walk with a friend, listen to your favorite music, or work on a project that makes you happy.

Consider Talking To a Professional

If you find yourself having trouble dealing with the loss, recognize that you can visit a counselor to help you through the loss.

A therapist won't judge you for expressing your feelings. They will encourage you to tell your story then they will help you develop strategies for dealing with the pain you are going through. Talking to a professional about everything is one of the fastest, most constructive ways to get back to your life.

Your children will soon become young adults, so consider setting the example you would want them to follow. They also grieve like adults do. Show them that it's okay to cry in the open, ask questions about death, talk about loved ones that have died, and to visit a mental health professional and discuss their feelings if the need arises.

You must demonstrate the importance of healthy coping mechanisms.

Don't Be Surprised By Unexpected Feelings

You probably considered the possibility of your parent's death for several months or years before their death. Your brain already understood the possibility of them dying at any time if they suffered from an illness for a long period of time or reached an impressive age. Even though your brain understood the possibility of their death, your heart refuses to understand the death. You can still feel a rush of unexpected emotions, so don't be surprised by the unexpected feelings.

The effect of the death may be lessened since you were already expecting the death. Their impressive age doesn't take away the pain you feel after their death. You had a unique relationship with your beloved parent during their lifetime; let them live on in your heart.

You may feel a mix of emotions if you were by your parent's side as their caregiver before their death. Relief is a normal emotion after the death. It's okay to feel that way, and this doesn't mean you are a bad person; it means you are only human, and you did the best you could for your beloved parent when they needed you.

Avoid blaming yourself for the ebbs and flows you will experience after your beloved parent dies because grief cannot be boxed into one feeling.

Offer Support to Your Surviving Parent

You will start paying more attention to the emotional needs of your surviving parent after one of your parents has died; most adults that have parents over the age of 65 help to ensure that their affairs are taken care of. They also help their surviving parent with the next stage of their life after the death of their spouse.

Discuss the idea of a caregiver stopping by to care for them. Discuss the idea of someone waiting on them to drive them to assignments, and even to the grocery store. Discuss issues that will help make their life more comfortable and what they plan to do with their time.

Accept Help And Ask For It

You may find yourself busy with many different tasks after the death of your parent. Be willing and ready to accept help from anyone who offers it; you don't have to do all the work by yourself. If someone offers to prepare a meal for your family or clean the house for you, appreciate their kindness and graciously accept their help.

Also, don't hesitate to ask for help. You need to learn to delegate some of the many tasks you have to do; this way, things will get done and fast too. It will also create room for friends and relatives to support you during this period.

Mortuaries often help with some arrangements like hotels, flights, and organizing receptions. Making use of your home for a reception or making flight and hotel arrangements don't have to be your responsibility.

Let Go

You may find yourself replaying disagreements and misunderstandings you had with your parent while they were alive and wondering what you could have done differently.

You may become too hard on yourself and get yourself worked up while blaming yourself for moving your elderly parent into an assisted living facility.

You have no choice but to be gentle on yourself. Acknowledge that you did your best during the period leading up to your parent's death. Let the guilt go one day at a time.

Mourning a Loved One

Since it is not easy to cope after a loved one dies, there is a natural process you go through after a loss, and that is mourning. Friends and relatives come together for mourning, and it may include religious traditions to honor the person who has died. Mourning a person can last months or even years.

Grieving, which is the outward expression of the loss you have suffered, can be expressed in different forms. An example of an emotional reaction is crying, while an example of a psychological expression is depression. Allow yourself to express these feelings.

People often avoid talking about death. Separating yourself from the pain may seem like the best thing to do at first, but you cannot run away from the pain forever. Someday those repressed feelings will come in full force, and you may end up falling ill because of it. Physical symptoms like loss of appetite, stomach pain, loss of energy, and intestinal upsets have been reported by many grieving people. Mourning can shake your body's defense systems, creating new illnesses for you or worsening illnesses that you may already have.

Sometimes people may get obsessed with the deceased. Suicidal thoughts, anxiety attacks, and chronic depression may arise. As time goes on, your grief experience helps you to cultivate and grow new skills.

While we grieve, we should reach deep into us to draw out the strength and joy residing in us. Let the wisdom we have acquired during our time of grief guide us on the journey of life without our beloved parent.

CHAPTER SIX
Vehicle for Growth

Give your grief a voice; let it speak out loud. You can do this through spoken or written methods.

Grief can be used as a vehicle for growth. It will help you discover the hidden talents in you so that you can share them with the world.

After doing self-inquiry, soul searching, and searching for answers spiritually; it is time to shift your focus to what kind of life you want for yourself in the future.

Let us discuss a few things that you need to know about grief as a vehicle for growth.

Troubles Gradually Improve You

Life is uncertain. It sometimes creates chaos that makes our world look bleak. On one of those days, you may say to yourself that you don't even want to try to improve your situation anymore. You may not have the zeal to move forward in your career because you think that life's chaos can destroy all you have worked for anytime. For you, life is crazy, and you won't let its unpredictability bother you anymore.

Learn to embrace the chaos, accept whatever life throws at you, and make it into something better. Just keep moving forward, no matter the situation. Take little steps even though the future is uncertain.

You may want to predict what will happen before you take any action. You don't need to overthink and analyze issues. Go ahead and take action and stop getting your mind overworked by thoughts of whether things will work out well or not.

Self-doubt arises in you because you don't want life to blindside you with chaos. You ask questions and may become too careful until you never take any step at all. Sometimes, life's chaos troubles you in a way that you won't even be sure if it's over or if it's still ongoing, but you can be sure of one thing, though; once the chaos is over, you will emerge a much stronger person.

Your scars are meant to remind you that you're a survivor. If you look closely at whatever you think has hurt you in the past, you'll discover the beauty in the ashes. It has made you better equipped for your present and future.

For grief to make you a better person, it has to wash you; you have to go through the worst to get to the best part. Suppressing grief will make you live a life devoid of real emotions.

Meant for Bigger Things

The potential to be great lies within you. The possibilities of becoming great are endless. Who do you really want to become? Do you want to become a more successful business person, a great philanthropist, a better spouse, or a parent? Think about the possibilities of achieving your dreams and contributing something valuable to the world.

The greatness in you will eventually find its way out if you accept the chaos and take those little steps you're afraid of taking. Because we are all unique, your uniqueness will shine through and impact the world positively.

Clarify What's Really Important and What's Not

Clarity comes when you embrace the chaos in your life. You see clearly what gives you joy and satisfaction. You may think you're lost and headed for a crash, but trouble and confusion have been known to open doors that lead to self-discovery.

The mind cannot focus on too many things at once; it awakens for the best result when you get clear on what is worth pursuing and what is not. At this stage, some people begin to care more about relationships and family, and less about money. For some, they start caring more about their health, and drugs or other self-destructive activities don't matter to them anymore. They gain clarity over what is important and what is not.

Picking Up the Pieces of Grief

You have walked through your own fire of hell; yes. The death of your beloved parent has shattered you to pieces but make it a practice to pick up the pieces of your life. You will see the passion for life awaking within your heart as you wear your pain as a badge of survival.

You won't be forgetting your loved one; you can laugh while missing them. You can live without them but still talk about them.

Take risks, fall and pick yourself up, and build your courage. You can dream and live again, and never stop loving your beloved parent.

Putting the Pieces Together After Life Falls Apart

Wake up in the morning and say to yourself, "*I will embrace my pain and make the best use of it*". Our journey of life is one filled with opportunities, changes, and adventures. Relationships are lost, and relationships are gained.

When life gets tough, we may be stuck in survival mode, thinking that that is the best we can achieve for our life, and we may not even realize it. We are so destination-oriented that we don't pay attention to everything that happens to us along the way.

Some of the darkest places in your life are the places where you will find more strength. When you come out of it, you will be better equipped to help people going through what you have been through.

When you create a new template for your life, you can still go back to your dreaming self even if you have forgotten the person.

Strengthen Your Grief Muscles

Our grief muscles can also be strengthened, just like our physical muscles. We may not even be aware that our grief muscles are being developed.

Every day you go without your loved one, and the things you learn to adapt to after their death is proof that you are learning to carry your grief while moving forward, and your grief muscles are being strengthened.

There will be times when the weight of your grief will be too much for you to carry. Forging ahead despite the pain, and taking one step at a time is what matters most.

Sometimes we get carried away by time-wasting activities that we don't pause to think about what matters most. The death of our loved one should remind us that life can be over any moment, so we should make the best use of our time here on earth.

There will definitely be times when you will be down, but your willingness to get right back up is what is essential for your life's mission to be accomplished. Looking at grief from different perspectives can help us improve.

Let us take a look at the reasons why grief can help you get better in your life.

1. **Valuable Lessons**

The grief we go through after a loss can help us learn valuable lessons. If we find ourselves in the same situation of despair, we will have gained the necessary experience and learnt the valuable lessons that will help us pull through. We will be well equipped to make better decisions than the first time we went through such moments of grief.

2. **Different Way of Looking At Your Relationships**

People will come into your life, and people will also leave. Our relationships with them will help us reevaluate our life and decide if certain people are helping us grow or if they are actually pulling us backward. Dramatic situations will reveal to us who we should continue to let into our lives and who we must let go.

3. **Discovering What Matters Most**

Letting go of unimportant things is best for us. Most times in life, we can fall into the trap of getting busy with unimportant things.

When we get busy with important things, those things that used to matter to us before will no longer matter. We succeed in giving less attention to unimportant things when we focus more on the things that matter most to us.

Grief helps us discover what matters most in our lives. Let's face it; if we don't know what matters most to us, we will end up wasting our time on irrelevant things. So, it is important that we take a step back to take stock of our lives to know our priorities and pursue what matters most to us.

Live as though you have a short time to live. If you had a short time to live on earth, what would you do with your time? Would you still be doing all the things you are currently doing, or would you retrace your steps to do something else that matters most to you? Pondering on this question will help you discover what matters most in your life.

4. **Appreciating life**

If we always remember that we have a limited time on earth, it can motivate us to make the most use of our time. We will appreciate life more, follow our passions, and work towards fulfilling our purpose on earth. Every day we live is a gift, so appreciating life will bring us the happiness we deserve.

5. **Helping others**

Sometimes, when we go through certain situations in our lives, it makes us open our eyes to our environment and the people around us.

We begin to notice the sufferings of those who are going through what we have already gone through in the past, and we decide to help them.

Many non-profit organizations have been created simply because they have experienced grief in the past, and were now being touched by the grief of others. Helping others and contributing to their lives will bring us happiness and fulfillment in life.

6. **Valuing memories and experiences**

Loss can make us remember things that have happened to us in the past. The memories of the past are an important part of who we are today. Valuing our experiences and memories of the past can shape who we become in the future.

We may want things to work for us just the way we want them to, and this desire can keep us from moving forward. Pausing and reflecting on our lives from time to time can help us make the needed changes that will make our lives better. We can then look at life from a different perspective.

Tough times have been known to bring out the best and worst in people. We can get angry and say nasty things to people when our temper rises. Reacting to issues quickly without pausing to think about it creates more problems.

Learning to press the pause button, taking a deep breath, and going for a walk when our disposition turns sour, is sure to restore us to calmness and peace.

Tap into Your Passions

It is great to talk to others about your experiences. As you do so, it will keep you motivated and help you find a reason to keep moving forward with your life.

I am sure you have some goals that you really want to achieve in your life. Remind yourself about your need to achieve these goals and stick to them. Be concerned about being the best you can be and achieving your life's purpose.

Your goals may change as a result of the death of your parent. That's no problem; it's perfectly fine. Accept and embrace the change. It is always better to move forward into an uncertain future than clinging to the painful events of the past.

Sit and ask yourself questions about how you want your life to be; then, take an inventory of your values, goals, and purpose. Ask yourself questions like:

What is my priority in life right now?

Why am I here? What is my life's purpose?

What is the vision I have for my future?

What goals do I need to set?

What will my Life look like if my goals are achieved?

How can I start working towards my future?

Remember to take one step at a time. When moving in a new direction, it's wise not to move too quickly or too early. Set aside time for relaxation and self-reflection. It's important that you build a solid foundation for your future goals as you take the needed steps to achieve them.

The following points will help you with your growth.

- Recognize that not all relationships in life are straightforward; some can be difficult. Learn to forgive yourself and learn from the experiences you have been through.

- Be the kind of person your parent would be proud of. If you have some regrets and feel like asking for forgiveness, write a letter addressed to your beloved parent. You can also write a letter back from them, expressing their understanding and forgiveness.
- It is advisable to find a counselor if the burden of grief is too much for you to bear, and it won't go away. You will find it helpful to attend bereavement support groups where everyone there understands the feeling of grief. There are many paths that lead to healing. You can also join a faith community where you will find solace.

Remember that you have to move towards your grief so you can heal from it. Grieving is not an overnight trip; it is a lifetime journey. Since grief's timeframe is different for everyone, ensure that you capture the good memories, treat yourself properly, strive to become the best version of yourself, and help others who are also grieving through their journey of grief.

Creativity as a Remedy: Coping With Emotional Pain

Creativity can be a remedy for your emotional pain. You can transform the emotional pain from the death of your parent into something beautiful if you use creativity to express your feelings.

Expressing your creativity is a really great way to explore your feelings. Creativity can help you open doors you never knew existed and hasten your healing process. It can help you understand yourself, and even your life better.

Learning and playing a musical instrument, writing songs and poetry about your feelings, or simply journaling your thoughts are helpful ways to express yourself.

You can also make drawings and paintings reflecting your feelings, or celebrating the life of your parent who has died.

You need to be easy on yourself and set yourself free. What you do doesn't really matter as long as you're allowing yourself to creatively try new things. You don't know what you may achieve with this. One thing may lead to another, and you may even discover something unique about yourself in the process.

Creativity has the power to change our lives. One of the best forms of healing that we can utilize is creativity. Following your passion will give your life a creative direction. It will help you heal and move on with your life.

Pain Can Lead To Greatness

Pain can motivate you to become great. Many of the greatest people in history were motivated by pain. We may not enjoy it while we are going through the process, but we need to embrace our pain.

Works of art have been inspired by suffering and pain, which is an inevitable part of life; many of these paintings have gone on to become globally known.

Breathtaking and haunting music alike have also touched us and helped us feel better in times of heartache and pain.

Movies, books, and performances have the power to penetrate our hearts and transform our pain into beauty.

Art Helps Artists

Artists strive to express themselves in the best way possible. Their art helps them deal with their emotional issues. Artists don't hide the powerful emotions they experience; they use them instead as inspiration to express their creativity.

We know that critically acclaimed and renowned pieces of art have been created out of pain's inspiration.

Everyone has gone through frustration and pain at some point in their lives. In a society where most people seem to be obsessed with happiness and positive thinking, an artist welcomes their fears and sadness and makes them into beautiful pieces of art. Art helps artists deal with their issues when the feelings are expressed through creativity.

We need to be as honest as artists so we can better channel our creativity into something useful.

Become an Artist Too

We all have creative power in us. It's a part of our human nature to be creative. Our thoughts have creative power; our words and actions also aid creativity.

Every calling has the opportunity for creativity. Even if you're a baker or a scientist, you can find your form of expression. Opportunities abound for creativity in every hobby or profession.

Look into yourself and check for what you are naturally good at. What do you enjoy doing without any stress? What seems to be pulling you?

Art can be created from everything. Express your creativity through your art and transform your pain.

Art has no limitations; it is freedom. You may not create a globally renowned work of art, but something that will help you get through your grief can be created.

Blueprint for Your Life

Are you happy with the life you are living now, or do you feel as though you have been moving in circles trying to get others to approve of your lifestyle?

We are all meant to craft our own lives, and this makes us all artisans in a way. We must take our future into our hands as we are responsible for shaping it. You are ushered into greatness when you actively create and follow the blueprint of your life.

Maturity means that you know where you are in life and where you are headed.

There are rules to follow for the plan of your life:

Decide what you want to do with your life and make a plan for it. Know exactly what you want to achieve each day, each week, each month, and each year. Write down your plans and stick to your vision. You are ready to move to the next level once you master the art of planning. When you break your plans into smaller parts to achieve, it makes it easier to see where you're going. Do something every day to further your vision.

We know that it is a good thing to be hopeful but hope alone will not get you there; you will need the discipline to achieve your goals. Once you have developed the plan for your life, your days, weeks, months, and years become a part of the long-term vision you have for your life.

Many people today just move in any direction life blows them to because they have no blueprint for their lives. Life just happens to them.

No one needs to know the plans you have for your life. You will understand the direction you are headed in better because you are planning all the steps you are taking.

Remember, you are the best person that can move your life forward. Creating and following the blueprint for your life will help to numb the sadness from your grief. As your life becomes meaningful, you will be happy again, less sorrowful, and filled with self-love.

CHAPTER SEVEN
Yet Another Holiday

After losing your parent, you may be dreading the holidays due to some family traditions that you may have practiced with them over the years. Their absence becomes pronounced, and it causes so much grief and unbearable pain because your beloved parent may have played an important role in your life and that of your family during the festive season.

We have said that it may take several years to heal from the pain of losing a loved one, while for others, the pain never really goes away. Usually, the first year spent after losing a loved one is the most painful and heart-wrenching.

Show me something more painful than heartbreak; it's actually the loss of a loved one. In the case of heartbreak, there is still that knowledge that your significant other resides somewhere on the planet, but they are just out of reach; there is still a possibility of reconnecting with them.

But in the case of losing a loved one to death, there is absolutely no hope of ever seeing them again, hence the pain. Spending the first holiday without your beloved parent, especially if you have always spent the holidays together, is usually your first face to face meeting with reality.

So, when it's time for the thanksgiving dinner, the Christmas family reunion, mother's day, or father's day celebrations, and the silence in their absence becomes much louder, would you curl into your shell and hide away from the rest of the world in hopes that your pains will fade away?

Would you sit still, enveloped by pain, or take proactive steps that will help you recover from the misery?

Surely there should be some form of coping mechanism to steer you back to reality and keep you from savoring the taste of sorrow when you watch the happiness of others remind you of your own misery.

In anticipation of the holidays or events that make the absence of your beloved parent pronounced, the best way to cope in such situations is to prepare against such days and adopt coping mechanisms that will be useful in helping you cope with the loss.

Grief Triggers

Apart from the holidays or special festive seasons, there are some other occasions that come to remind you of the absence of your beloved parent; such occasions could be their birthdays, their wedding anniversary, or other special occasions.

Having these reminders is absolutely inevitable. Your pain doesn't magically end with these events always hanging around the corner, and bringing to mind all the wonderful memories of the beautiful times you spent with your beloved parent.

Sometimes things such as music, the smell of cologne, certain sounds, and some environments could make you remember the loss of your beloved parent. You will always be overwhelmed with emotions anytime you drive past their favorite barbershop or their favorite restaurant.

As you journey towards your healing, there will always be reminders or grief triggers. It is actually a natural process that you must go through on the way to your healing.

When Grief Rears Its Ugly Head

It may seem like reminders are always waiting in hiding, looking for opportunities to show themselves to you; they just won't leave you alone.

What do you expect when grief rears its ugly head?

We have said that you will always be flooded with emotions during the holidays, anniversaries or when an event, place, or situation reminds you of the loss of your parent.

Sometimes, you may think you are actually beginning to get over the loss until you come across one of these grief triggers or reminders. You turn around and begin to question your ability to heal from the pain in your heart and actually get your life back when the emotions come pouring in like it did on the first day the news of the death of your beloved parent came to you.

Such returning emotions could last for days or perhaps, longer, and you may find yourself re-exhibiting one of the following emotions or character traits:

- Fatigue, tiredness or lack of energy
- Disinterest in regular or daily activities.
- Insomnia
- Severe depression
- Anxiety
- Fear
- Loneliness
- Feeling of emptiness
- Guilt
- Fatigue

- Deep pain
- Regret
- Feeling of worthlessness
- Desire to stay indoors
- Drunkenness
- Oversleeping
- Overeating/loss of appetite
- Suicidal thoughts
- Abuse of drugs

These reminders or triggers could suddenly bring to your memory what you have already forgotten or what you are struggling to forget. It may bring to mind in great detail the activities that surrounded the death of your parent, and it could lead to a sudden outburst of emotion, uncontrollable anger, or depression.

While some people may decide to bask in regret or become controlled by a wave of negative emotions, the coping mechanism of some others could be the simple act of trying to sleep away their depression. Falling into a deep sleep for several hours may provide you with a temporary means of escape from your pain, but the pain will resurface the moment you wake up.

So, how do you get over the loss of your parent when your child, who looks exactly like your deceased parent is stuck with you forever? You are bound to always come across triggers such as festivities, anniversaries, or places of interest of your parent? There may also be photos, clothes, or accessories of your beloved parent hanging around somewhere that creates sharp pains in your chest whenever you see them; you get beautiful memories that suddenly leave you in tears.

There are tips to help you heal and cope with grief during holidays, and they include:

Preparation

Now that you know that there will always be events that remind you that your beloved parent is gone forever, will you allow the associated waves of negative emotions to control your happiness every time you see a reminder, or will you manage the emotions?

You need to make preparations for any reminder that may try to increase your pain. When you are prepared for whatever may come your way after the loss, you will be able to manage your emotions when a reminder suddenly catches your attention.

Practicing Mindfulness

To prevent your emotions from getting the best of you during the holidays or anniversaries of your deceased loved one, you have to take into cognizance the thoughts, places, or events that cause you sorrow in connection to their death.

It would be easier to manage your emotions when you can detect the switch in your emotions and the events that cause this sudden change in emotions. In a situation when you come across a grief trigger, you will do well to fix your thoughts on something more exciting and exhilarating.

Get a Distraction

After taking note of the events or places that evoke negative emotions in connection to the loss of your loved one, the next thing to do would be to get a person or event that would serve as a form of distraction to prevent you from suffering the effects of grief triggers. You could hang out with friends or loved ones to prevent you from becoming lonely and sad.

Focus On the Good Memories

Rather than focusing on the loss and the pain of having to live life without them, focus on the good times shared and all the great qualities or character traits of your beloved parent; this would bring smiles to your face, and you won't become depressed from the fear that you will never see them again.

Practice Gratitude

Focus on being grateful for the opportunity you had to share life with them and how they may have impacted you and every other person they came across; this will help you heal quickly, and you will have a different point of view regarding the loss. Realize that our deceased loved ones are always with us; this may not seem true at the early stages of grief, but in time, this reality will sink in. You may not see them, but they are closer than you think. You will begin to feel and hear them through the voice or words of strangers, kind gestures, your dreams, and others around you. Then, you will realize that the dead never truly leave us. They are a part of us forever.

Do Something in Honor of Your Parent

You could start a foundation or non-governmental organization in honor of your parent. You could also carry out other charitable activities in their honor. Such activities could include scholarships, annual visits to an orphanage home, annual donations to a charitable organization on the birthdays of your deceased parent, or you could plant a tree to tackle climate change in their honor. When you become busy with these activities, you will feel a bit better, and it will ease your pain. It will give you a sense of fulfillment and encouragement that your beloved parent would be satisfied and happy with you wherever they are.

Play Their Role

If your deceased parent had a specific role that they played in the family, it would be an honorable thing for you to step into their shoes and begin to play the role they played in your lives while they were alive.

Such roles must not be challenging but should be something easy, convenient, and within your power. They can be something as easy as taking your kids to the park to play during the holidays if your deceased parent used to do that, or taking your kids to school and bringing them back. It can also be you stepping in to bear the financial burden of raising a relative whose parent is deceased; this will help ease the pain of the other people your deceased parent left behind. It would be an honorable thing to do this because the responsibilities of the deceased, especially roles played by them during the holidays if left unattended to can cause more sorrow and pain.

Get a Support System

You can get connected to your close friends, relatives, and close friends of your beloved parent. You would be able to share your grief and speak to people who genuinely understand how you feel.

Also, social groups, bereavement groups, and spiritual leaders will be of immense support. Having people around, especially during festive seasons or periods of the anniversaries of your deceased loved one, will prevent you from having suicidal thoughts, and it will keep you from being lonely.

Talk to a Psychologist

A psychologist or therapist will avail you the opportunity of emptying out your emotions while being guided on the best possible ways to heal from the pain. These individuals are trained to help people recover from grief or any other form of emotional trauma.

You can obtain their services by visiting their offices and booking sessions or gaining access to them on social media. There are countless therapists and psychologists on social media, and it is quite easy to obtain their services. You won't have to worry about booking sessions, driving long hours to meet with them, and you won't also have to worry about speaking to someone who has no idea about what you are going through.

There are various psychologists, and the prices for their services vary. You can get one, depending on what you can afford. The services of some of these therapists may not come cheap, but it will be well worth it.

Allow Yourself to Grieve

It is advisable to allow yourself to grieve after the death of your loved one. Mourn your loved one properly as this would hasten the healing process.

Ensure that you don't bottle up the tears. Allow the tears to flow freely. It is actually therapeutic to cry when you are feeling any emotional pain of any sort, so release the emotions. Let it all out. After the flow of tears, be sure to get yourself back up and move on.

It is Okay to Have Conflicting Emotions

Having conflicting emotions is normal during mourning. Allow yourself to feel and express different emotions. It is a part of the healing process. Keep in mind that it's a festive period, and it should be a period of joy, laughter, and happiness. Engage in things or spend valuable time with people that will make you happy.

New People

During the period of mourning, it is essential that you go out and meet new people. Make new friends and spend time with old friends; this will help keep your mind from excessive worrying over your deceased parent. It may not necessarily numb your pain or make you completely forget your loved one because you can never find their replacement. It is, however, advisable to meet new people so that you can find a new reason to smile again.

New Hobbies

It will be erroneous and suicidal to constantly remain indoors while wallowing in grief and self-pity. You may develop new hobbies or keep yourself busy with the old hobbies that you already have. Activities like sports, swimming, writing, and drawing are excellent choices that can be considered. Keep yourself busy with whatever kind of hobby makes you happy; it will help you take your mind away from the events that surrounded the loss of your parent.

Jogging

Jogging helps speed up your heart rate and may help get rid of depression. In addition to helping you stay fit and healthy, this activity will take your mind off the loss of your loved one, thereby reducing the pain you're going through.

A Local Gym

It is a good idea to obtain a gym membership from your local gym during the festive period. Do not shy away from doing that. Joining the gym nearest to you will help you meet new people and make new friends.

Apart from meeting new people that may help you feel better and become happier, joining a gym will give you the opportunity of using the gym equipment to work out, and this is beneficial for your overall wellbeing. Just like jogging, other forms of exercise such as squats, bench press, press-ups, and sit-ups, help you stay fit; they are great for your mental, emotional, and physical health.

Work On Your Career or Pursue Your Dreams

Holidays or festive season may be a period of rest, fun, or a period of getting together with family and friends, but there is nothing wrong with working on your career or pursuing your dreams. If you have a vision or specific work-related plans, you must start working on them as this would help you take your mind off the death of your loved one and the loneliness you feel during the festive period.

If you want to start that NGO, write a book, get a new job, start up a business or produce a movie, you can take advantage of this period to start it as it will occupy your mind and prevent you from being enveloped in sorrow when you think about the loss of your loved one.

A New Skill

A new skill will occupy your mind and help keep you focused on something other than the death of your loved one, thereby reducing the effect of grief triggers. By giving you something new to think about, it will keep you from dwelling on the death of your loved one during the festive season.

In addition to that, you will look back and see that the death of your loved one helped you become a better version of yourself by learning a new skill.

Work On Your Attitude or Personality

If there is a part of you that you are not proud of or a personality trait that your deceased parent had always complained about, you can take steps to work on them. Practice patience if you were a bit impatient. Practice selflessness if you were selfish, and try to become more organized if your loved one had complained that you were a bit unorganized.

You can make up your mind that you are doing it in honor of your loved one, and this will relieve you of the pain as you will begin to see the death of your loved one from a different perspective. Each time you look back and remember their death, instead of holding on to the pain, you would view it as a turning point in your life, a period where you reevaluated your life and made positive changes in your life.

You will be able to say, the death of your loved one made you a better person instead of being completely negative about it.

Give It Time

Time, they say heals all wounds. This statement may sound cliché, but it is actually true. The way you felt when you first heard the news of the death of your loved one would be completely different from how you would feel about the loss after about one or two years.

So, if you feel devastated, cry yourself to sleep every night, or you feel so empty such that you feel there is nothing left to look forward to, and you have nothing to live for, be encouraged, and give it time; this too shall pass. The pain will slowly fade away. During the anniversary or festive season, you may be feeling so much pain, but remember that this too shall pass, and you will surely smile again.

When Grief Becomes Overly Intense

While time helps to lessen the grief, there is, however, no time limit to grief. So, in a situation where a lot of time has passed, and you are still not able to heal from the pain caused by the loss of your loved one, it will be advisable to contact a therapist or a psychologist to prevent the occurrence of severe medical conditions such as high blood pressure, mental health disorder or even death.

CHAPTER EIGHT
One Day at a Time

Living your life and taking it one day at a time is one of the best ways to get over the loss of a loved one. It is one of the best advice anyone out there can give to an individual who has recently lost a loved one. The living your life and taking it one day at a time approach is often employed by therapists and psychologists when helping an individual get through the emotional trauma suffered from the loss of a loved one.

Many people who are suffering from the loss of a loved one may be burdened by fear, which often leads to overthinking, depression, and various medical conditions. The key to avoiding falling into depression is learning to handle the death of that special someone by taking it one day at a time.

Getting over the death of your beloved parent may appear difficult, especially if you were very close to them during their lifetime. In this case, many people focus on what may happen in the long run, thereby putting a lot of pressure on themselves instead of living life one day at a time.

Many bereaved individuals dread what will happen in months or in a year from when the death occurred, and it could be because of the following reasons.

Financial Burden

Your deceased parent might have been responsible for providing financing for some things and thinking about the huge financial responsibility left for you to carry its weight might cause you more pain and emotional trauma.

In this case, don't focus on the new financial responsibility that the death of your loved one has placed on you, and the financial implication in the long run. Instead, learn to tackle whatever financial issues crop up one day at a time; you will see that things will be gradually taken care of, and the trauma will not break you.

Loneliness

Many people are afraid of living their lives without their loved ones; this fear may become heightened when there is a sudden death of that special someone in their life.

The key to tackling this problem is imagining that they have gone on a trip and would be back. Should your parent inform you that they were going on a trip, would you be depressed because they were going on a trip? I don't think so.

People often place their focus on being left alone without their loved one for so long; this causes them more trauma. To prevent being enveloped in grief, put your focus on learning to live without your loved one, one day at a time; the fear of not finding someone who will love you as much as your beloved parent may be deeply rooted in your heart.

So many people put unnecessary pressure on themselves when they are mourning their loved ones.

People often hold on to the idea of being attached to their loved ones forever. They are closed-minded towards other people, so when they get the rude shock of the death of their loved one, they become devastated. You should be open-minded about making new friends and meeting new people.

Have it in mind that your life is not tied to any individual, and you can actually live without them; this may be a bitter pill to swallow as you may not have been able to think about the idea of living your life without your beloved parent present in it.

Practicing the act of taking each day as it comes helps you realize that your life is tied to no one, and life just has to go on after the death of your beloved parent.

Tips to help you take the death of your beloved parent one day at a time:

Break Large Tasks into Smaller Ones

Even though it may seem like your world is now standing still, the death of your parent does not automatically stop every other activity in your life; life goes on. You still have your career to pursue, kids to cater for, and lots more.

Your deceased parent may have always been there to assist you, but don't let their absence make you lose your will to live. It may seem overwhelming having to go through the pain and also carry out your daily activities.

Thinking about how you can survive the pain of the next day will only stress and hurt you. You should learn to focus on what each day has to offer.

Focus on small tasks at a time. Break your large tasks into smaller ones that you can focus on each day. Focusing on smaller tasks each day will reduce your stress, and you will notice that you are able to achieve your goal or complete great tasks by doing smaller things.

Do you want to know the step to take to simplify your tasks and divide them into smaller tasks? Take a look at the next point.

Practice Journaling

A lot of people do not fancy the idea of writing. Putting things down may seem quite boring to a lot of people. Writing what you plan to do each day actually helps to simplify your work. It also gets rid of stress.

You can break down monthly goals into smaller daily goals by writing out what you intend to achieve each day.

Obtaining a diary to pen down your thoughts is also a fabulous idea. Learning to put down the thoughts going through your mind actually helps you heal; writing down emotions has been said to be therapeutic and improves mental health.

Journaling can be done daily as it will help you stay focused on a particular activity. When you have noticed a considerable improvement in how you feel, you can re-schedule your writing to once a week, during the weekends, and subsequently during festivities, anniversaries, and special occasions.

When a loved one dies, especially at the initial stage, there tends to be a lot of activities that need to be done. Thoughts about how to go about everything may be running through your mind all day, making your mind chaotic as you may be focused on activities that need to be carried out in weeks or even months.

Practice making lists as it will help you declutter your mind and de-stress your brain. You won't have to think long and hard on what needs to be done, as everything that needs to be done will be reduced into a little list; such lists should be made daily.

Meditation

Meditation is a powerful tip that helps you handle the loss of a parent one day at a time. Meditations, especially if done daily and correctly, can help you get through each day without depression.

Meditation should be done in a quiet environment. The best time of the day to meditate is usually in the mornings. Meditations can also be done at night to speed up the effects. It helps to clear the mind, improve focus, and it also helps to prevent or stop depression. Studies have shown that meditation improves mental health.

For effective meditation, keep your eyes closed and ignore every distraction. Let your focus be on your breath for a few minutes; breathe in and breathe out to help you relax. After that, gradually begin to focus on happy thoughts. It could be the goals you intend to achieve or happy memories; doing this daily will help you gradually get over the loss of your beloved parent.

Practice Affirmations

Affirmations are statements usually made with a sense of confidence or strong belief. They have the power to reprogram the mind to believe a particular truth. They are usually said to remind you of something or an idea which you are beginning to lose sight of.

When you lose your beloved parent, you may begin to lose sight of reality by focusing on the lies your mind tell you; these lies may include thoughts like, "you will never find happiness again; it's the end of the world for you; you will never get over the pain".

These are mere thoughts, but you might give them power and turn them into reality if you continue focusing on them and letting them run through your mind all day. Thoughts are powerless until you give them power by affirming them constantly.

When you keep speaking negative words, you bring them to life, and before long, you may find yourself stuck in a cycle of grief.

Practicing affirmations daily during the time of your grief can actually heal you and help you get over the hurt. Affirmations can be practiced for about 10 minutes in the morning, afternoon, and night of each day.

You can use positive and uplifting words like:

- *I am strong*
- *I am doing just fine*
- *I am getting better and better each day*
- *I choose to focus on my goals*
- *I will conquer this pain*
- *I choose to focus on positivity*
- *I choose to focus on beautiful memories*
- *I choose to focus on my blessings*

These words may seem insignificant, but they work. They may not appear to be effective, immediately erase the pain, or change the situation, but if repeated over time, they would produce the right results.

In a situation where you feel your words don't yield much power or show any results, you could employ the services of a therapist to help you with these affirmations.

As humans, we tend to believe the words of other people over our own words or thoughts. When we were children, we often hung on to words of affirmations from our parents, teachers, family members, and friends, whether they were positive or negative. The beliefs that came from those affirmations set the tone for our lives. Your positive affirmations may be powerful, but that of a therapist could be way more powerful and effective.

Apart from employing the services of a therapist for your affirmations, you can also write down your affirmations repeatedly until they begin to get into your subconscious mind, and eventually become your reality.

Use Your Vision

To get over your loved parent, visualize the travails of a mountain climber. While climbing a mountain, they do not focus on their previous step, neither do they focus on the many steps to be taken before getting to their endpoint; they take it one step at a time knowing fully well that focusing too much on the end may discourage them.

Looking down may also make them feel dizzy as they might be engulfed by fear while looking at the depth of the abyss. The mountain climber looks not to the left, the right, up or down; they just stay focused on each step they take. In the same way, focus on surviving each day, and you will come out stronger, for it is said that ''yesterday is gone, tomorrow is not promised''.

Therefore, you should focus on the day that you are sure of, which is today.

What happens when everything fails, and your pain won't go away?

It is allowed to mourn and feel every negative emotion. It is, however, advisable to know the different stages of grief and to determine if you have been mourning for too long. It also forms part of the healing process. But after some time, you should get yourself back on your feet and begin to live life and smile again.

So, when everything fails, and your pain won't go away, your best bet would be to take one step at a time.

CHAPTER NINE
When the Glue Is Gone

Most times, when a father or mother dies, the family falls apart.

A family is often kept together by their co-relationships to the head of the family. Once the head of the family dies, a distance is created between the other family members. Everything falls apart like a house of cards when the glue that kept the family together is gone.

The family may struggle with staying together because the father or mother may have had some unique qualities, making it difficult for any other family member to step into their shoes.

The falling apart is avoided by some families; these families already have members of the family taking on increased responsibilities when their parents are still alive. They acknowledge the fact that their aging parents won't be with them forever, thereby taking practical steps to share in the duties of their parents.

They start following in their parents' footsteps when they are still alive. A family member may start overseeing the kitchen activities, and another may start making the needed calls that keep the family organized and in unity. Practice makes perfect; as they continue to handle these activities, they become better at them.

At a time when everyone is devastated by the loss of a loved one, family conflict can often overshadow grief.

After a parent passes, death brings out the best and worst in the family. You are going through the grieving process where you are trying to cope with the death of your beloved parent. Suddenly, your support system feels like a source of additional stress instead of giving you support.

Families fall apart, but you are certainly not alone in this. Many people have experienced conflict after the death of their parents; they can relate to what you are going through.

Reasons for Conflict

Family conflict after the death of a parent is common. The behaviors of some family members change when the person they strive to impress the most is no longer on earth.

Let us take a look at the reasons for the conflict.

Hidden Long-Term Issues

Dormant rivalries between siblings can be revived after the death of a parent.

There may be some issues between the family members that have been hidden for a long time; they may have been coping with these issues while their parent was alive. Since the parent kept the family together while they were alive, their death may cause conflict between the siblings when these hidden issues raise their ugly heads.

Grudges from the past can become fresh in their minds, and they may end up going to court over something that can be resolved at home.

Money and Property Issues

Death on its own is agonizing; the pain of heir warfare doesn't have to be added to it. Fighting over a deceased's inheritance is an ugly business.

After the parent who is the financial pillar of the family dies, the living family members may be pushed into battle with the fear of financial security. They find themselves at odds over the dead parent's material possessions; they start fighting over the deceased's estate if they died without leaving a will. Money and property issues are a major cause of conflict between the living family members after the death of a parent.

At this time, the family members would benefit more from leaning on each other's shoulders. Unfortunately, misunderstandings grab them and pull them apart at a time when they should be holding each other's hands.

When there is no will for guidance, money quickly becomes an issue when it is being put together for the funeral; it also becomes an issue when the deceased's investments and money in the bank accounts are being divided.

Some of the deceased's belongings will not be accounted for in the absence of a will. Even when there is a will, the family members may still fight over sentimental items.

Their family may be one that has never been known for materialism, and they also never give up their values for money or gifts. So, it becomes a thing of surprise to them. All of a sudden, they start arguing over stuff they never wanted or even cared about when their loved one was alive.

It may be hard to admit, but countless families have found themselves engaging in disagreements and fighting over their parent's estate and material possessions.

The beautiful family bond that a parent leaves behind after their death is the most valuable part of any inheritance. Remember that what matters at the end of the day is that bond; stuff will only be stuff.

Is It Just About The Money?

Sometimes, a combination of things may be responsible for the family members fighting over their loved one's money and property.

Even though money may be harder for many people to come by now, holding on to their loved one's wealth may not be their main desire; there is an unconscious desire for them to hold on to their loved one.

So are they fighting just because of the money? I honestly don't think so.

They may want to cling on to something that will always remind them of their beloved parent; they want to have something that they will treasure forever. Desperately holding on to their loved one's possessions fulfills their desire to hold on to the person.

Missing Efforts

People may not put in the efforts they used to put into attending family events when their parents were alive. They may withdraw into their shell while dealing with their own grief and that of others.

Let's take a look at this scenario: Dad died some years ago, and then mom also died last year. After the death of mom, family members begin to make excuses as to why they can't make it to family gatherings. All of a sudden, they become too busy to attend family thanksgivings that used to bring them close.

You are greeted with a cold silence whenever you mention it via your social media post or on the phone to any of your siblings.

In the absence of your mother, the truth suddenly stares you in the face. The beautiful family bond that you have enjoyed all your life is gradually fading. You begin to realize that your beloved mother was the glue that held the family together. You start asking yourself questions about how you can keep the family together when your mother, the matriarch of the family is gone. Many families have experienced this.

Family members gradually start going their separate ways, and old traditions are lost while new ones are formed. Even though you may find yourself always longing for the connections you had with your family members when your mom was alive, the bitter truth is that you may never regain it.

However, all hope is not lost; let us discuss some helpful information that you can carry along on your journey through this process.

1. Each family member is different, and their grieving methods are also different. Instead of addressing their grief, they may choose the path of avoidance. In this case, family events are avoided with the intention of running away from the pain their loved one's absence will cause them. The avoidance approach may

seem to be working for them at the moment, but the long-term effect of it is prolonged grief.

2. The family may have been kept close due to activities involving them caring for their aging parents. They may want to keep their beloved parents happy and make their last days memorable. Every family member is free to move in the direction they want to move in. So, when their parents are no more alive, they move on with their lives. New traditions and new ways of celebrating holidays are then birthed.

3. You don't have to give up on the connections you share with your other family members; you can still involve them in your new traditions and ways of celebrating holidays. Send out invitations to them when you have something to celebrate and lend a helping hand to anyone in need of it. Even though the other family members may have moved on with their lives, they can still respond positively to your

invitation.

4. Change things around. What worked for your beloved parents may not work for you, so try new things. You may fail at trying to re-create the hosting of the holiday events exactly the way your parent used to do it. It will be evident that someone is missing. Trying to become exactly what they used to be, and failing at it may bring stress upon you.

5. You can still make your beloved parents a part of your events without them being physically present with you. Remember the times of laughter, and don't deny the younger generation of stories about their grandparents. The important thing is to remember the good times shared with your deceased parents, and not to increase your grief by dwelling on the fact that they are no longer with you.

Don't stop trying to keep the family together. Keep reaching out to your family members and extending invitations for events to them. Enjoy a good time with whoever shows up, and don't hold a grudge against who doesn't. Be nice about it. They may simply not be ready to be reminded about their deceased parent, so respect their choice when they don't honor your invitation. They might just show up the next time you invite them, so keep trying; giving up should not be an option for you.

The Time to Begin Sorting Through the Deceased's Belongings

Some family members may want to sort through the deceased's belongings immediately, while others may want a little more time before doing that. Misunderstandings resulting from arguments about when to sort through the belongings can spring up.

Disagreements over What to Keep and What to Give Away

There may be disagreements over what to keep and what to give away. Some family members may display a higher level of attachment to their late mom's belongings than the others. While one family member may be keen on having them keep all their late mom's items, including containers, another may insist on throwing those items away.

Disagreements Over Keeping A House or Not

Houses are valuable possessions. Selling off a house bought by a deceased parent can bring in a huge amount of money. Many family members are sentimentally attached to the houses owned by their parents, and they will not want to part with them; they will want to keep them. On the other hand, many others are concerned about the financial stability the sale of the houses would bring them, so they will want to sell them off for financial gain.

Disagreements about the End of Life Treatment

Some families start experiencing conflict even before their beloved parent dies. Sharing caregiving responsibilities, disagreement about certain goals, and hospital needs are some issues that may cause strain and conflict amongst family members.

Funeral Arrangements

Conflicts can also arise during the funeral arrangements; issues such as the place where the funeral service will be held or the place where the person will be buried may cause conflicts between the members of the family.

Relocating After the Death Occurs

It is common for living family members to relocate after the death of a parent or loved one. They may decide to move out of that region to another region. When some family members relocate, the family can be split geographically, and this move can be devastating for the family members left behind in that region.

Grieving Styles

People express grief in different ways. Grieving styles may include not only sadness, but also indifference, or unexpected lack of emotions; these behaviors can surprise the relatives and friends of the bereaved.

When people grieve differently, it can be a major source of conflict in the family. A family member whose grieving style is sadness may think another family member whose grieving style is indifference is moving on too quickly after the death of their loved one and may get annoyed about it.

Coping With Family Conflict

Unfortunately, there is no easy way to have all conflicts resolved, but here are a few suggestions to help you cope with the conflict in your family.

The Brain

Stress makes the brain function differently. You have parts of your brain that think more on emotion and impulse, and you have parts that think rationally.

It is difficult to think with the rational part of the brain during trauma, so the emotional part of the brain is used in such situations.

When people under stress interact with each other, they do this from a place of emotion, thereby leaving room for conflicts to occur.

Control

People may be threatened by a loss of stability and control when they experience the death of a loved one.

During the grieving period, they may do things like trying to plan the funeral all by themselves without input from the other family members. They may also make the decision to sort through the deceased's belongings.

All these are done by them in a bid to regain a sense of control.

If a family member seems to be creating room for strife while trying to regain control, you can help that person have a sense of control. Talk to them about the problems their actions may be causing for the other family members; the family members can then help this person to channel their energy into doing things that would be useful for the family.

Communication

Communication is an important factor in reducing conflict. Lack of proper communication can lead to conflict between family members. Adequate arrangements should be made for who does what, the time to do certain things, and how certain things will be handled.

The time to go through the will should be agreed upon so that everyone can be present. Everyone should also be carried along while discussing the next steps to take. There should be regular communication between the family members to ensure that no one is left out of the plans being made.

Effective communication is vital at this stage as everyone is going through the grieving process. Try to give feedback about actions that have been taken and stay on track. It is best to focus on working together as a team.

Accusations should be avoided at all costs. Instead of using "you" statements, use "I" statements. For example, instead of saying, "you threw away mom's shoes...you are so thoughtless...", you can say something like, "I was really hurt when you threw away mom's shoes without first talking to me about your decision. I felt like you didn't care that I was attached to those shoes."

The "you" statements are non-productive and tend to backfire; they can lead to arguments. People always respond to them in defensiveness or shame. Their response would be something like, "I am not... I did not...". They can also become offensive after feeling defensive, saying something like, "you are the one who...". It will be difficult for you to win such arguments. The "I" statement is a game-changer; it can help us avoid disputes.

By focusing on how the person's actions made you feel, instead of accusing them, you can create room for dialogue without making the person become defensive. Listen carefully to what they have to say, so you can both reach a resolution.

Always remember that effective communication is crucial if you want to avoid conflict, and work together with the members of your family.

Be Gentle and Forgiving

By all means possible, try not to generalize the negative behaviors of others. For example, you have known your cousin for many years, but become irritated by a wrong action that they have taken during the grieving period. You may feel that the person has changed after your loved one's death and is only concerned about getting ownership of the deceased's car or some other property. You may feel like you are now getting to see them for who they really are. Don't become too fast to call them greedy and condemn them.

Sometimes, grief makes us do crazy things that we may later regret. One wrong action of a person during the grieving period shouldn't make you forget all the wonderful things the person has been to you throughout the 15, 30, or 40 years that you have known them. Take this as an exception in the person's behavior, not the rule.

Be gentle and forgiving with yourself and others.

Mediation

There are trained professionals that you can reach out to if you are unable to manage the conflict on your own. They can work with your family during the period of grief and help you avoid conflict by helping you all better understand each other.

Remember the following things, if you find yourself in conflict with family members after a death occurs.

Remember the Context

Remember that everyone is grieving and going through stress at this time. Arguments are normal during the grieving period. Grief can be challenging.

It can make people display frightening and complex emotions.

Feelings like sadness are common, but anger and irritation are also feelings that you should expect at this time. The funeral arrangements and matters concerning the deceased's estate are issues that can put everyone under stress.

Don't Make Assumptions

Don't make assumptions about what your relatives may be thinking. Discuss issues and share your views. Your opinions may be different from theirs, so talk openly and let everyone have the opportunity to express their feelings. You may think everyone feels the same way about how the funeral should be organized, but you may be wrong about that; they may not share your views. It is wise to discuss issues before taking important steps.

Remember that everyone grieves differently, and loss can bring out different emotions from people, so do not judge them if they grieve differently from you.

When family members question the way you're handling the death of your parent, try to act calmly and not getting defensive or angry; it is essential that you have supportive people in your life during your time of grief.

CHAPTER TEN
When History Is All You Have Left

One of the biggest challenges you will face after the funeral is trying to figure out what to do with all the stuff that your parent left behind.

You will have to sort through all of their clothes, shoes, bags, and other items. It is a difficult stage because you will have to make difficult decisions about the items to keep and the ones to give away or donate to charities.

It can be excruciatingly hard to decide which things to keep and which things to give out. Your mind will be filled with a million questions. Should you keep their journals, gym equipment, childhood photos, books, or shoes? If you are moving to a new house, you'll be wondering which of the things you will take with you to your new home. The reality is that you can't keep all of their stuff; you will have to do away with some.

Sorting through their property can be a work in progress; it can leave you physically and emotionally exhausted. Preserving your loved one's memory will require you to make use of some practical and creative ideas so that you don't keep stuff that you don't need.

When someone close to us dies, we may think that our connection with the person is over. We sometimes think that the best thing to do is to try to let go of the person's memory and forget all about the person, but we never really get over a terrible loss that easily. We don't have to force ourselves to forget all about them because we are trying to get over our grief; you can still honor them and remember them in unique ways without bitterness.

People have different mourning styles, and these styles change as time goes on, but the relationship you had with your beloved parent is never really over. It never dies; it lives on. You still carry them in your heart.

You can make your loved one's memory a treasure; there are creative ways to do that. Holding on to happy memories of your parent honors their life and the special bond you shared with them. It also helps with your healing.

We all know that losing a loved one is one of the most challenging and heartbreaking events that will ever happen in our lives. We haven't lost everything we love about our parent even while death deprives us of being with them physically. What happens is that we move over from physical relationship with our loved one to a relationship based on memories.

The journey through grief is not a straight path; it is a meandering way that is filled with many steps. Along the way, it involves going back to revisit our memories so that we can move forward toward our healing.

Our beloved parent may have left this world physically, but their memory doesn't have to die, too; we can still keep it alive.

Apart from the ceremonies you perform to honor your beloved parent after their death, there are other creative things you can do to honor their memory. You may be interested in preserving your loved one's memory but may not know what to do.

There are creative and thoughtful ideas for honoring your deceased loved ones. Below are some wonderful ideas that you can consider.

Memory Photo Book

Put old photos of your parent into a special book so that you can share those memories with family and friends. Even though albums consume a lot of space, it's not easy to throw photos of your loved one away. Making a photo memory book out of your parent's photos taken during sports events, holidays, or memorable outings is an exciting idea.

Another idea is to select some favorites out of the pictures and scan them into a digital memory book. Upload the pictures to your preferred site, choose the layouts that appeal to you most, or use their premade templates. The book can be viewed online, and you can order a copy of it.

Since bulky albums take up a lot of space on bookshelves and in closets, this method is effective in helping you store your loved one's photos without having to keep bulky albums at home.

Flipping through the pages of the book will stir up loving memories. You can even keep their memory alive by handing the book down to the younger generation as a memory book.

Pillow or Quilt

You can sew a pillow or quilt from your parent's clothing to help you feel their presence.

For a loved one who was an athlete, piecing together a T-shirt quilt using their favorite T-shirts from sports events is a great idea. It can be displayed or even passed down to the younger generation in honor of your loved one's athletic achievements.

Sewing special memory pillows will make you feel good. You can select your loved one's favorite shirts and use them to make pillowcases. When you sew them and slip pillow forms inside, they can serve as something that you can hold onto when you miss your loved one. You can also write unique phrases on them such as "this used to be my shirt, remember that I will always love you."

You can work with individuals and companies that specialize in providing this service if you can't do it yourself. They are skilled at it; they will help you make the pillow and quilt using your loved one's clothing.

Memory Box/Memorial Video

You can make a memory box that is filled with things that will keep your parent's memories alive. You can work with the little ones when assembling a memory box.

A wooden box or even a shoebox can be used for the memory box. The outside of the box can be decorated to make it look beautiful. You can write your parent's name on it, or you can paint it in beautiful colors.

Special items like jewelry, photographs, or a favorite pen can be put inside the box. Look for things that bring back positive memories. The memory box will remind you of the good times spent with your loved one.

The funeral is a great place to start this. You can ask relatives and friends to write down their tributes or stories about your parent that they would love to share. They can also bring a memento of their relationship with your parent. You can then add items such as letters, cards, or other treasured items to create a memorial that will be long-lasting.

Since children's memories fade over time, a memory box or memorial video will be helpful for them. Your children can watch the videos whenever they want to. They can also hold onto the items in the memory box; this will help them form a connection with their grandparent who has left this world.

Memory Garden

Something about nature is fresh and beautiful. To honor your parent, you can plant a tree or a memory garden. It will be beneficial to the earth, and you will also have a place to sit, meditate, and enjoy the gift of nature.

A Piece of Art

You can make a piece of art for your parent and commission it.

Light a Candle

You can light a candle and place it next to a photo of your parent on days that were special to the both of you; doing this ritual will make you feel close to them, even though they are no more here with you.

Special Giveaways

Organize special giveaways where you give things out to people. You will be happy when you know that you are giving things out to people who actually need them.

You can donate some things to charity, and also give out some truly special items to people that are close to you like your relatives and friends.

Giving them those items will make them feel blessed to be the recipients of the special items.

Frame a Letter

After a loved one's death, we are particularly happy about meaningful things that they shared with us during their lifetime.

Your beloved parent may have shared something meaningful and interesting like a motivational letter, or a love letter from your grandfather to your grandmother.

It may even be your parent's recipe or notes about bible passages. It doesn't have to be something grand; it just needs to be something you hold dear to your heart. Framing your parent's letter or recipe is a creative way to honor their memory.

Framing a recipe or letter is also a great way to showcase your beloved parent's handwriting.

Most people think that recipes are just instructions on how to make something, but they also tell a story about the maker of the food. Recipe cards that your loved one left in their handwriting can be framed as art and displayed in your kitchen.

You may need to learn from mom's secret sauce recipe or that special cookie recipe soon.

Decorating the Home with Books

Books are a great way to tell the story of a person's likes. You can use your parent's books to decorate the home. Old books can be used to decorate the home; this recent trend in home decoration is great for decorating the home with some of your loved one's favorite books. You can also choose to place the books in a glass case if you don't want fingers staining them.

Save Pictures and Documents on a Drive

Your loved one's pictures, videos, and even

documents may be stored on different devices; put them all on one hard drive. You never know if they'll be important to you in the near future.

You can share your parent's legacy with your children and maybe even grandchildren; this is a great way to preserve treasured files.

Handwriting Jewelry

To honor your beloved parent's memory, you can use some of their items to create unique jewelry.

You can use their pearls to make bracelets and earrings too. Unique pieces can be created from items like gears from clocks, and from guitar picks also.

You can take something that has been handwritten by your parent and contact vendors who can make it into jewelry for you. Scan your parent's actual signature or handwritten words into the computer and send it to the jewelry company; they will engrave it into a piece of jewelry for you. They will artfully make a beautiful gift with a message that is written by your beloved parent.

You will have something unique once a creative jeweler incorporates something special that your beloved parent once owned into the jewelry they are making for you.

You can also create this special piece yourself.

Magical Box for Your Kids

You can create a magical box for your kids by placing some objects in a small box so that they can play with it. You can include stuff that you find valuable and don't want to do without. The box can contain items like your parent's gloves, glasses, and money clips. Let the kids play with the box and mention the person who once owned the items.

A Refuge/Memorial

After your parent passes away, you can decide to create a refuge in your backyard. You can put some chairs. You can also create the refuge indoors if you want.

It will be a place for you to go to spend some time and think about them. The place where you create the refuge doesn't really matter. What you need is just a quiet place that you can go to think about your beloved parent.

Setting up a permanent memorial and visiting it regularly is a great way to honor your beloved parent. During your period of grief, you can go to a place where you feel the closeness of your loved one. You can make their gravesite the special place you visit to feel close to them. You can also plant a memorial tree or install a memorial bench at a particular place so that you can visit that place from time to time.

Passersby will be touched by your beloved parent's life if you include a memorial plaque.

Acts of Kindness

Do some random acts of kindness for people in memory of your beloved parent. You can do something like baking cookies for people or any other act of kindness.

You can choose the ideas you like or get creative with your projects; these acts will make you feel better.

Your beloved parent may have many collections of extraordinary items, and it may not be possible for you to keep them all. You can just select a few of them and have the rest shared amongst relatives.

Your relatives will appreciate them and display them in their homes.

Celebrate Your Parent's Birthday

Your beloved parent has passed on; the first birthday after their death can be painful to you, but you can also make it a special time to honor their memory.

What you can do on their birthday every year is to take a few moments to be thankful for the life they lived and the many ways they impacted your life. You can look back on the love and support they gave you, the wisdom they shared with you, and all the happy moments, and honor those memories by sharing all your beloved parent has taught you with others.

Dinner in Their Honor

You can honor your parent's memory by hosting a dinner in their honor.

Pick a day that is special to them; it could be a special day like their birthday, anniversary, or even mother's or father's day. You can then arrange for the dinner and send out invitations to friends.

The dinner can be held at your parent's favorite restaurant, or you can select dishes that they really enjoyed for the dinner. Share the memories with your friends, and they will be there to support you.

Get Involved With Organizations

A great way to honor your parent's memory is to get involved with an organization or charity that your parent favored. When you do this, you are continuing their legacy.

If they were not involved with any organization or charity, you could think about their passion and what they loved to do. Consider providing school supplies to kids who need them if your parent was a teacher and loved school kids.

Another thing you can do is to volunteer your time to ask about the upkeep and see to the maintenance of a park they enjoyed walking at. Did they volunteer their time at a local soup kitchen? You can also do the same and invite your friends to join you in volunteering.

Create Your Own Tradition

Creating your own tradition is another excellent way to honor your loved one's memory.

You can make it a tradition to watch the kind of movies they enjoyed watching on their birthday. You can also make it a tradition to read the kind of books they enjoyed reading once a year in honor of them.

Did your parent love a particular fruit so much?

Let's say they loved bananas; set up a day where you invite friends to an evening of banana-flavored foods. Every meal served will be flavored with or served with banana. You can serve foods like banana bread, strawberry-banana smoothies, or banana pancakes.

You will have a wonderful evening with your friends and in honor of your beloved parent too.

Special Places

You can continue visiting the special places that you and your parent used to visit together. Did you have a favorite vacation destination or a favorite coffee shop? Visiting those places after their death will help you remember them. You will also have a good time in the process.

It is also a great idea to write your loved one a letter each time you visit those special places. In the letter, tell them about the times you visited those places with them, and tell them how much you miss them not been there with you.

The death of a loved one doesn't mean you should forget them entirely. It doesn't take away the love you have for them; the love remains. The relationship you shared with them shouldn't be forgotten; it's worth remembering, so share the memories with others. It is important to note that your relationship with your loved one doesn't end after their death. Your bond with them can continue to be cultivated throughout the years. Continue to honor their memory and still keep the conversation open even long after their death.

Even if you're not yet ready to sort through your loved one's belongings, it's okay; take your time. Endeavor to do what makes you happy.

You need to express your feelings, and these activities will help you do that well; the activities will make you feel closer to your beloved parent and help you move forward in your journey through grief.

It takes time, and lots of backward motion before forward motion occurs.

CHAPTER ELEVEN
Grief and Spirituality

The relationship between belief and grief is worth discussing at this stage in your life. Let us talk more about it.

Questioning one's faith is completely inevitable when a loved one dies. However, people react differently in such situations. In times like that, some people may lose their faith, or have it challenged, while some others may have their faith fine-tuned.

We are all spiritual beings and leaning towards the spiritual part of our lives when we lose a loved one is a necessity.

Since most people question their beliefs when a loved one dies, while some others have their beliefs strengthened, it is wise to ask the questions that come to your mind and not to bottle up your feelings.

You can find someone like a spiritual leader to guide you and help you strengthen your belief. A person's belief or faith can be of great help in times of grief as it can provide some form of comfort that everything happens for a reason, and you will be alright.

How Can Your Spirituality Help You Through Grief?

The loss of a loved one can be a bitter pill to swallow, and the process of grief can be tough, but what is tougher is the fact that being spiritual does not prevent us from losing a loved one or going through the process of mourning, because death is a natural part of life.

Your spirituality may not prevent you from losing a parent, but it could help make the healing process faster. Although we may not all be religious, it is believed that we all are spiritual beings. It is, therefore, vital that you pay attention to the spiritual side to aid the healing process.

Spend Time Alone With Your Source

Every religion has a supreme being, which they look up to or refer to as the Maker. This being is often a source of help, protection, and support to them.

Spending time in prayer to your Source could help alleviate your emotional pain and make you feel better.

In the early stages of grief, you may find yourself disappointed, or you may begin to doubt the very existence of God. Asking questions like does God exist? Does he care about me? If he does, why would he let this befall me? Questions like these can draw you further away from your faith. It is absolutely normal to feel this way even though many religions preach that in all things, we should give glory to God.

All your concerns can be clarified in the place of prayer, so, instead of wallowing in grief and letting the pain weigh you down, you could go to a quiet place and spend some time in prayer with God. Some people often travel to a lonely place where they can have some peace or even lock themselves up in a room for days or weeks, not necessarily mourning but in prayer and communication with God. While you may not get answers to your burning questions, spending time in prayer to God will help you heal, and you will come to discover his burning love for you.

You will discover that the loss of your parent happened for a reason, and he alone understands why it happened. If you trust him with your healing process, he will not only heal your broken heart and make you feel loved again, but he will take the place of your deceased parent, and do better the job of a father or mother than your deceased parent could have ever done.

Believers Mourn Too

Some faith-filled individuals believe that people of faith or spiritual people are not allowed to grieve. Some religions believe that people deep in faith should not mourn because, to them, mourning is for the unbelievers. Some people allow these thoughts to sink into their subconscious, and they may begin to think that their level of grief shows the depth of their faith.

People may make you feel like an unbeliever for mourning your loved one. They may tell you that there is no need to mourn because your loved one is with God. When you are first informed about the death of your parent, you may be shocked, or you may continue to live in denial. Living in denial of the death of your parent may slow down your healing process; this may lead to depression or a mental health disorder in later stages.

It is advisable that you get a grip on yourself and accept your parent's demise as it is the first step towards healing. A lot of people may not accept the death of their loved ones and may begin to search for various spiritual means on how to bring their loved ones back to life. In most cases, this step had failed and only ended up creating more spiritual problems and slowed down the healing process.

Crying is not weakness. Crying when suffering from emotional pain or due to the loss of a loved one, is recommended as it aids the healing process. Bottling up of emotions and holding back tears could destroy the bereaved by causing mental health disorder or depression in the long run. The hurt might remain with them for a long period of time.

So, it is totally acceptable to cry; let the tears flow freely because crying is therapeutic. Being a spiritual person, you may believe that there is something called an afterlife where you will reconnect with your loved one and live happily ever after, but it does not change the fact that you are bereaved. The pain will be there for some time, so each time you feel the tears, let it flow.

Since grief is normal, you shouldn't feel like an unbeliever for mourning your loved one. When you feel those negative emotions, let them flow because they will help you heal, but after pouring out your emotions, know when to let go and move on.

Read the Holy Book

Study the precepts of the holy book, depending on your religion. You can search for passages that have to do with how to manage grief.

The various holy books have passages on how to handle grief. For example, the holy bible says in Romans 34:18 that ''The LORD is close to the brokenhearted and saves those who are crushed in spirit''. Also, Psalm 147:3 says, ''He heals the brokenhearted and binds up their wounds''. Another important passage for those in mourning is Matthew 5:4, and it says, "Blessed are those who mourn for they shall be comforted".

Reminding yourself what God said concerning the loss of a loved one could be a source of renewed hope knowing fully well that God knows your pain, and he is closer than you think.

In studying the holy books, you may get to understand what happens to the soul of the deceased after death.

For many people who are bereaved, they fear that their loved ones will seize to exist, and they can't imagine life without them. Reading the holy books may help you understand that your deceased is still with you, watches over you, and still prays for you. You may find that comforting in your time of grief.

The holy books of different religions have a record of what happens after death. Having such knowledge might comfort you and enlighten you about the role you are to play after your loved one dies.

According to the holy bible in the apocryphal book of Esdras, a certain young man named Ezra was informed by the Angel Uriel about what happens to the soul after death. He was given two accounts; one is about those who die without salvation, while the other is about those who die with salvation.

It was said that when a person who lives in sin dies, his body returns to the earth, and his soul returns to his maker. He goes through some form of torment before witnessing the glory of his maker; seeing his maker is only meant for him to be covered in shame and regret.

Also, when a person lives a good life, his soul returns to his maker, and he beholds the glory of his maker first before being allowed to witness the events happening after his demise. He would be allowed to see how his relatives react to his death, his rewards and habitations will be shown to him as well.

This passage makes us understand that the dead are not really dead. They see, and they hear us. Knowing this should encourage a bereaved individual, and it would help such a person to act according to how the deceased will want them to.

A deceased parent may want his daughter to be brave and courageous. He may not want the son or daughter to be completely broken by their death, but to pick themselves up and gradually get over the loss.

The account of what happens in the afterlife varies with different religions. If you are a person of faith or a spiritual person, finding out what your religion teaches about death, and how to get over your loss will aid the healing process a great deal.

Holding on to your faith, spiritual beliefs, and asking questions about the dead would also help. It may be difficult to understand because of the confusion and emotional pain, but keep believing that everything will be alright.

Deal With the Feeling of Guilt

Feeling guilty is absolutely normal when a person is mourning, but what isn't is when a person allows the feeling to linger for a very long period of time. There is no need to feel guilty over the death of a loved one. Instead, you should be encouraged as a person of faith, knowing that there is a chance that you can reconnect with your loved one.

Getting rid of this feeling may be difficult, so to help you with this, you should give yourself the advice you would give to another grieving individual. Ask yourself what you would say to them if they begin to feel guilty after the loss of a loved one. What would you say to them if they feel like they would have done things differently to prevent the death?

They might also be feeling guilty if they had not rendered enough help to the deceased, or if they never spent quality time with them when they were alive. Figure out all the kind and comforting words you would say to them and take your own advice.

Constant self-criticism will hinder your healing process and may lead to depression. It is of great importance that you learn to forgive yourself for whatever grudge you hold against yourself concerning the death of your beloved parent.

Faith-Based Practices

Traditional faith-based practices could be a source of

strength to you in your time of mourning. Those practices could be a regular visit to your place of worship to attend church services and also to stop your mind from being focused on the grief. In various religions, there are different practices or rituals that could be made in honor of the dead.

In the Catholic Church and other Pentecostal Churches, masses or church services could be done in honor of the deceased; this will bring a sense of peace and inner joy knowing that you are doing this to please the dead or to favor them.

In some religions, it is advisable to pray for the dead as it is said that it will assist them in the afterlife.

Silence During Grief

When people are bereaved, too many thoughts may be running through their minds at any particular time; you may be bothered about a lot of things ranging from how to plan the burial, what to expect as a result of the demise, or the pain of not having your parent around.

Having an overactive mind during the time of grief may lead to severe medical conditions such as high blood pressure and may even cause death. In the time of grief, it is advisable to be quiet in your mind. Let go of all the worrying about what the future holds and focus on the present.

Having an overactive mind could also lead to appetite loss and extreme weight loss, which may cause dizziness and nausea often. In this situation, one important thing you can do is to practice mindfulness. Whenever you are about to think thoughts that will cause you to be distressed, change your focus, and begin to practice gratitude.

At this point, you may be thinking there is nothing to be grateful for because you can't find anything positive in the situation. You are required to search for something to be thankful for. You could start by expressing gratitude to your source for making your paths cross with that of your loved one. Be grateful for their personality and for their achievements during their lifetime.

Your mind will be taken off all the negative thoughts going on in your mind; it will make you feel better. Much of the pain during grief does not always come from the knowledge that your loved one is gone; the pain you suffer is usually because of the constant thinking and worrying about the issue.

You may sometimes begin to experience high body temperatures and constant headaches as a result of the overthinking. Body pain and eye swelling are also bound to occur from too much crying.

Instead of crying, take solace in the fact that they have returned to their source or maker, and of course, you cannot love them better than their maker.

Work On Your Anger

We have said that anger is a normal process of grief. You may find yourself being angry at your source, relatives, friends, or even yourself. When this happens, know that it's a normal process, and there is nothing to worry about.

At this point, take out time to find out why you are angry with yourself. Could there be something you feel you could have done differently? Are you mad at people because you think they could have prevented the loss or treated the deceased in a particular manner, but they didn't? Perhaps, you might be angry with someone who happens to be the cause of the loss of your loved one. Find out the cause of your anger and find a solution.

You must understand that everything happens for a reason, and staying mad at your source, yourself, or other people won't bring back the dead; instead, it will cause confusion, despair, and bitterness.

Talk To Your Spiritual Leader

You may be suffering from confusion and utter disappointment following the death of your loved one, and a million questions may be running through your mind; you will need answers from a spiritually knowledgeable individual.

Your best bet will be to talk to your spiritual head. He or She may not necessarily provide all the answers, but they will provide the most suitable words of encouragement for you.

They may also pray for you or perform some religious rituals that will help you heal and also help the deceased in the afterlife.

Pray For the Deceased

Almost every religion requires some form of prayer for the deceased. If it were not necessary, simple statements like, ''May their soul rest in peace'' will be completely invalid and won't be made in honor of the dead. During the time of mourning, after mourning and all throughout life, it is advisable to always pray for your deceased loved ones.

Apart from helping them in the afterlife, it will also keep them in your memories. Praying for the deceased brings a certain kind of fulfillment.

Now, the question is, what do you pray about? You can pray for the repose of their soul. Many religions believe that some souls roam around the earth instead of returning to their place of rest for reasons such as; death at a young age, unfulfilled dreams, violent causes of death, or they may have a piece of information to pass to a loved one. Therefore, praying for them will help them return to their place of rest.

Almost all religions believe in what is called "the judgment day'' and the idea that one's deeds, whether good or bad, will be recorded by a higher authority, to be either used against them or in their favor on the day of judgment; this idea differs amongst the various religions.

In some religions, it is believed that when a person dies, their soul immediately returns to their maker for judgment. Some other religions believe that the soul of the deceased will seize to exist until the day of judgment when every dead person will rise to be judged and rewarded according to their deeds.

Some religions believe that there will be eternal damnation for those who committed evil during their lifetime. Eternal punishment can come in various ways, which include; being thrown into a lake of fire, having demons torment such souls forever using whips, thorns, or other sharp objects.

For members of the Catholic Church, it is believed that there is a place called purgatory where the souls of the dead who committed venial sin (minor sin) while alive can purify themselves and become fit to enter heaven. It is believed that the prayers of loved ones on earth for the souls in purgatory will help hasten the process of purging them of their sins and their transition into heaven and eternal rest.

Make Room for Healing

By now, you know that grief is a normal part of mourning, but wallowing in it for too long is suicidal. It is time to let go. Take it upon yourself to heal emotionally. Be open to healing and change.

Allowing yourself to heal after the demise of a loved one is no easy task. It requires a lot of work internally and externally. Every single day, you should take deliberate steps to heal.

Take the steps mentioned above to heal and get over the loss of your loved one. You may have gone through grief, but that does not mean you should stay down. Refuse to wallow in self-pity, shake the pain away, and get your life back together.

In Everything, Give Thanks

In everything, give thanks. What you are going through is going to heal someone tomorrow. Don't be cheated out of your opportunity to thank God.

Listen to songs that describe your situation and offer you hope; they will help you when you feel down. Choose songs that will lift your spirit. Avoid songs that make you feel more depressed about your situation; they will not lift your spirit.

When you keep complaining about the situation and feeling depressed, it will not help your situation.

Gratitude helps us to remember the good things God has done for us. Be deliberate in your choice to show gratitude.

CHAPTER TWELVE
The Other Side of Grief

The death of a parent can be life-changing even though society often sees it as a natural occurrence. You feel the hurt and pain, but some others only see it as a natural thing for your parent to die.

Life should be cherished. You can still enjoy your life even without your beloved parent. They would be glad that you are happy, and you are making the best use of your life.

You may feel like life cannot go on without your parent, but there will be light at the end of the tunnel if you embrace your grief and look on the brighter side of life.

Unlocking a New Chapter

Unlock a new chapter of your life where happiness will be your normal.

If you have lived long enough on earth, I'm sure you would have seen the endings of some major eras in your life. Try to look on the brighter side even if you don't want to.

Yes, we know that the loss is difficult to bear, but strive to be a positive person and not a merchant of gloom. Life isn't selective; it makes bad things happen to good people too.

It almost seems like some people have the gift of looking on the bright side of things, no matter the situation they are going through. But some others who have made negativity their bosom friend seem to delight in fishing out all the things that are wrong in the world; they always see a problem where others see an opportunity.

With this mindset, things almost always go wrong for them. Have you ever being with a negative person who always has something to complain about? They can be energy-draining; don't allow the hands of grief to mold you into that person.

There are things you simply can do nothing about, no matter how hard you try. So, make things easier for yourself by looking at life from a deeper perspective, focusing on the important things, and letting go of unimportant things and the things that you can do nothing about.

Problems come to help you grow as a person. Let the sun shining above the clouds always remind you to look on the brighter side of life, and things will get better.

Know that life is a book with both happy and sad chapters, but you can't just stick to one sad chapter and remain depressed; you need to turn the page to see what the next chapter has in store for you.

Whatever life throws at you, take it, and learn from it. Whatever you go through in life doesn't really matter; what matters is what you do with whatever is thrown at you. If your life seems to have been thrown off its course, you just need to take the necessary steps to get your life back on track.

If you're still struggling to adjust to the present reality of the loss, please loosen your grip on the past because something great awaits you. As you take the needed steps, you will gradually journey through your grief until you get to the other side.

Conclusions

There is an essential lesson wrapped within the situation you are going through.

If your beloved parent died from sudden death, you must have been struck by the realization that tomorrow is promised to no one, and knowing this can keep you on track. You will focus on what is important and not get lost in pursuing unimportant issues of life.

After experiencing the sudden death of your loved one, you begin to appreciate life more than you would have ever done if you hadn't experienced their death.

No one in their right mind would wish to have such tragedy befall them to teach them a valuable lesson of life; it doesn't feel good to lose a loved one.

Even though you sure can avoid troubles, they come to make you learn the needed lessons for your life. After you have overcome the troubles, you will understand why you had to go through them.

Every wound has a scar, and every scar tells a story. Grief is like a wound. A wound bleeds when it is still fresh, and then it becomes a scar after it has healed. It no longer hurts when it heals and leaves a scar behind.

Grief is just like that; after your healing, you no longer have painful memories of your beloved parent. You remember them with thankfulness that you had the opportunity to be a part of their lives. You no longer feel the pain like when they first died. You look forward to being with them someday.

Leave the pain of the past behind and move forward with the wisdom gained from it. Keep in mind that you will need to walk through the darkness to get to the end of the tunnel, where you can see the light.

With time, you will get over the loss of your beloved parent as you follow the steps outlined in this book.

Say this to yourself: Tough times don't last; tough people do.

Printed in Great Britain
by Amazon